CHILD CUSTODY

Also by Marianne Takas

CHILD SUPPORT

Marianne Takas

☐ CHILD ☐
CUSTODY

A Complete Guide for
Concerned Mothers

PERENNIAL LIBRARY

HARPER & ROW, PUBLISHERS, New York

Cambridge, Philadelphia, San Francisco

Washington, London, Mexico City, São Paulo

Singapore, Sydney

Grateful acknowledgment is made for permission to reprint: Listings of "References to the UCCJA, Criminal Parental Kidnapping Laws" and "Parent Locator Service in Every State," from the handbook *Parental Kidnapping* (August 1985). Reprinted by permission of the National Center for Missing and Exploited Children.

FIRST EDITION

Designer: Ruth Bornschlegel

Copyeditor: Marjorie Horvitz

Library of Congress Cataloging-in-Publication Data
Takas, Marianne.
  Child custody.
  Includes index.
  1. Custody of children—United States. I. Title.
KF547.T35   1987   346.7301'7   86-45699
                    347.30617
ISBN 0-06-055038-4   87 88 89 90 91 MPC 7 6 5 4 3 2 1
ISBN 0-06-096129-5 (pbk.) 87 88 89 90 91 MPC 7 6 5 4 3 2 1

For my mother, Jane Heath Takas, with love

Contents

Foreword   *ix*

1 □ WHAT MOTHERS NEED TO KNOW ABOUT CHILD
CUSTODY   *1*

2 □ GATHERING YOUR STRENGTH   *17*

3 □ WORKING WITHIN THE LEGAL SYSTEM   *31*

4 □ DEVELOPING A CUSTODY PLAN   *53*

5 □ DEVELOPING A FINANCIAL PLAN   *70*

6 □ CUSTODY AND SOCIAL CONTROL   *86*

7 □ PROTECTING AGAINST DANGER AND
INTIMIDATION   *100*

8 □ WHEN NEGOTIATION FAILS   *128*

9 □ BEGINNING TO HEAL   *148*

Notes   *151*

Appendix A □ Recommended Reading   *156*

Appendix B □ Legal Advocacy Resources   *158*

Appendix C □ National Networks for Self-Help
Resources *160*

Appendix D □ References for Use in Kidnapping
Cases *163*

Index *167*

Foreword

During the summer of 1979, before my third year at Emory Law School in Atlanta, Georgia, I learned of a pressing community need. Several local organizations, including a Legal Service office, an ACLU office, and some women's service groups, had contacted the law school with a similar request: Could we find a way to offer basic legal information and referral to Atlanta area women in need? Each of the concerned groups was being swamped with information requests they simply could not meet.

That was the beginning of the Emory University Center for Women's Interest Law (CWIL), of which I was the first director. Acting under the supervision of faculty member Nat Gozansky, we offered a telephone hotline information service and an ongoing lecture and discussion series.

We quickly found that family law issues were of the greatest concern to the women we served. Child support enforcement, child custody and visitation disputes, and battering by husbands or lovers were the problems most commonly experienced by our callers. Many were women not quite poor enough to qualify for the federally funded Legal Services, but clearly not wealthy enough to spend freely on a lawyer. Others had lawyers, but felt in the dark and excluded from the legal process. All needed basic information about their rights and about the legal system—much more, we soon found, than we could give them over the phone or in a one-day seminar.

Over the next several years, after I'd finished law school and entered the legal field, I found the same theme repeating itself. Working for a court handling divorces and other civil and criminal matters, I noticed that many women felt—often correctly—that they were being excluded from the decision-making process. Those who were being victimized at home (and therefore were in the greatest need of legal protection) often seemed to be the least effectively served.

Concerned about the problem, I agreed to serve on the legal advocacy committee of a local shelter for battered women and their children. I soon learned that women who sought legal protection from violence but experienced a poor response were often left feeling more endangered and more afraid for their children than before they had sought help.

The women best able to avoid this vicious cycle were those who'd learned enough about the legal process, including their rights and their options, to effectively advocate for their own protection. It was no panacea, for the legal system had and has serious gaps in coverage, but it was clearly an important start. Knowledge, it seemed, was the first step to empowerment.

At about the same time, I was contacted by a group of parents, mostly mothers, concerned about poor child support enforcement by the courts. These women also recognized that protecting themselves and their children meant understanding and advocating within the legal system. These women, too, saw that knowledge was power.

It was in response, then, to a widespread demand for practical information that I began to write. Hoping to reach as broad an audience as possible, I began with widely available magazines such as *New Woman, Cosmopolitan, Working Mother* and *Vogue*. By this time, I had left Georgia and moved to Massachusetts, where I was saddened to learn that the problems of access to and fairness within the legal system seemed to be just as severe.

In fact, I learned as I researched my articles, the problems were epidemic throughout the country. The California study of Drs. Lenore Weitzman and Ruth B. Dixon, now published as Weitzman's *The Divorce Revolution* (The Free Press, 1986), clearly established the devastating financial impact of the legal system's inequities upon divorcing women and their children. Other research, including work by attorney Nancy

Polikoff, psychologist Phyllis Chesler and others, focused on harmful and discriminatory custody policies.

This book is the second of two efforts to fill the information gap that helps to keep women at a disadvantage within the legal system. My first book, *Child Support*, focused on the financial factors of divorce and single parenting. This book emphasizes the interpersonal process of providing for your children's welfare after a divorce or family separation. Both are designed not to advise but to empower: to help you to make more balanced, informed decisions.

This book does not stand alone, but springs from a community of thought on women, marriage and divorce. Many of those whose work helped to develop the field were kind enough to share their time and insights with me. Several became valued friends as well. I am therefore deeply indebted to Carolyn Kastner of the Center for the Support of Children; Joanne Schulman, formerly of the National Center on Women and Family Law; Lillian Kozak of the NOW-NYS Task Force on Domestic Relations Law; Guinilla Jainchill of Harvard University Medical School; Nancy Polikoff of the Women's Legal Defense Fund; Judith Hermann of Harvard University Medical School and the Women's Mental Health Collective of Somerville; Richard Neely, justice of the Supreme Court of Appeals of West Virginia; Judith Wallerstein of the Center for the Family in Transition; David Adams of EMERGE; and Sheryll Kerns Kraizer, child educator and author.

In a twist of fate that may seem ironic, I have spent most of the past two years divided between two projects, both close to my heart. Professionally, I have been writing a book concerned with divorce and family separation. Personally, I have been growing happily in love and, last May, was married.

The irony is only an apparent one. In fact, I see a positive relationship between those two facts in my life. To me, this is a book less about divorce as such than about loving family responsibility. As I've talked with divorced and divorcing women, I've learned a great deal about strength and sensitivity under extreme stress. When I've heard anger, it's been an anger of self-respect and concern for the children, not one of bitterness or hatred. "I'm a good person, and my child is a wonderful child," that anger says. "I deserve fair treatment, and my child deserves love and stability."

At the same time, my relationship with my friend and husband, Ed Warner, has educated as well as delighted me. I've always believed that any system which draws lines between people—which accords privileges and power according to arbitrary facts like who is male or female, white or black, heterosexual or homosexual, and so on—is a barrier to good relationships. Fortunately, Ed and I share a committed desire to knock down those barriers whenever possible. That, combined with his intelligence and his loving nature, has been a real joy to me.

In a similar vein, thanks must go to my family and friends, who have loved and encouraged me through thick and thin. If I have energy to give my work, it's due to the loving support I've been given. I am also grateful to Diana Finch of Ellen Levine Literary Agency and Sallie Coolidge and Ann Martin-Leff of Harper & Row for their continued assistance and support of my work. Author Robert Phelps deserves special thanks for his kind encouragement of me as a writer.

Finally, my deep thanks go to each of the many women and men who shared their lives, thoughts, feelings and ingenuity with me as they discussed their family lives after divorce. In a very real sense, this is their book.

CHILD CUSTODY

1 | WHAT MOTHERS NEED TO KNOW ABOUT CHILD CUSTODY

Officially, in every state, child custody is determined on the basis of "the best interests of the child." That's as it should be. As a parent, you often have to put your children's needs first. You don't decide whether feeding them is what you really want to do each day. You feed them because they need to eat.

A child's need for a secure, stable custody plan may not be as obvious as the need to eat, but it's almost as essential. Divorce or family separation is even harder on children than on adults.[1] They see the center of their world falling apart, and they're too young to have an adult's confidence that all will work out for the best. Often, they feel anxious, angry, lonely, and depressed. A stable custody plan can do a great deal to reassure them.

The purpose of this book is to help you to help and protect your children during a difficult and painful time. It is written for mothers who are facing a possible divorce, are already divorced, or have never been married.

You may wonder why this isn't a book for mothers *and* fathers. In fact, the problems and conflicts typically faced by mothers during a divorce or family separation are very different than those faced by fathers. Sadly, our legal system today makes it very difficult—at times even dangerous—for a mother to protect her children's welfare during a divorce. The official goal of deciding custody based on the children's best interest is often not followed. For that reason, concerned mothers need information about the specific problems they and their children may face.

Although public awareness about these problems is increasing, there are still many myths and misunderstandings. It helps to look at some of those myths and at the cold, hard facts.

MYTH: Women automatically get custody of the children. Men who want custody don't have a chance.

FACT: Most men do not seek custody, but if they do, they are actually more likely than the mother to get it. In a recent major study, 63 percent of all men who sought custody of their children at divorce time did succeed in getting it.[2]

This wouldn't be disturbing but for the fact that in most families, the mother is still the primary caretaker* in the child's life from infancy on. While most fathers love their children, generally mothers are the ones with primary responsibility for child raising. Even if both parents are employed, mothers tend to be the ones who stay home with the children until they're old enough for day care, stay home from work when the children are sick, and wake up during the night to feed or care for them.

In 1985, for example, a nationwide survey showed that most married men whose wives were employed full time admitted that their wives did all (24 percent) or most (42 percent) of the household chores.[3] In 1980, advertising surveys showed that men were still resistant to child care duties and wanted most in a wife "a good mother who would assume responsibility for the children."[4] Actual studies of family dynamics offer an even bleaker picture: Most fathers spend little time in direct, interpersonal interaction with their children, although they may serve as group leader or disciplinarian.[5]

MYTH: If a man wins custody, it's probably because he is an unusually active and involved father, and may be as close or closer to the children than the mother.

* The term "primary care*giver*" would be more accurate, since concerned parents give rather than take care. Also, "caretaker" seems to reflect the traditional notion of children as property, since we usually associate caretakers with houses or other properties. Nonetheless, because "primary caretaker" is a technical term in the legal field, it is used throughout this book to avoid confusion.

FACT: There are certainly some fathers today who are as involved in child raising as their wives. Possibly, these men are less likely to be divorced, or if they do divorce, they may be more likely to work out shared custody arrangements. In any case, they do not fit the profile of the average man who wins custody.

In fact, most fathers who win custody were not particularly involved in child raising during the marriage. Often, what distinguishes them from the child's mother is that they earn more money, can afford a nicer home or neighborhood, and are ready and able to remarry quickly.[6]

According to Justice Richard Neely of the Supreme Court of Appeals of West Virginia, a man who wins custody will not, in most cases, go on to assume day-to-day responsibility for the child's care. Instead, he turns that duty over to a new woman: his own mother, a paid housekeeper, or a new wife or lover. (That woman has no custody rights, incidentally, nor has the child any right to continue the relationship with her, if the father later wants to end that relationship.) It's what Nancy Polikoff, director of the Child Support and Child Custody Project of the Women's Legal Defense Fund, calls "the theory of interchangeable mothers—the idea that any one woman will do as well as any other to care for any given child."

Ironically, it's probable that the father best suited to having custody of his children—the rare man who had been the primary caretaker of the children since birth—would actually be *less* likely than a more traditional man to win custody. Like the many mothers who sidetrack their careers to raise children, he would be less likely to be wealthy and powerful, the factors that most often help fathers to win. So the standards commonly used may act against loving and involved parents of both sexes—which is certainly against the best interests of children.

MYTH: If a woman loses custody to a less involved father, it's probably because she's been neglectful or abusive. Good mothers don't have to worry.

FACT: Very few mothers lose custody on grounds of being unfit, and most have been the child's primary caretaker right up until the custody dispute. Frequently, judges note that the mother has a close and loving relationship with the child or children, but they decide on other grounds.[7]

MYTH: As long as the children receive good care, it's not that important which parent gets custody. It may be unfair to the mother when a less involved father gets custody, but it probably won't hurt the child.

FACT: It is well known among mental health experts that a child's emotional attachments are crucial to emotional health. If a child is separated from the person who has been primarily responsible for caring for the child since birth, serious harm and pain will be inflicted. Even if the new caretaker has many positive qualities, the child will continue to experience depression, loss of self-esteem, inability to trust, and difficulty establishing new close relationships.[8]

It should be stressed that, while the role of the primary caretaker is most crucial, both parents are important to a child. Children whose fathers don't see them regularly after a divorce suffer a real sense of sadness and loss.[9] For that reason, concerned parents should work, whenever possible, to develop a custody plan that involves regular contact with both parents.

MYTH: Joint custody is the perfect answer to custody conflicts, because nobody loses.

FACT: Joint custody can be an excellent choice for two loving, involved parents who have the resources required to make it work. It is not, however, right for every family.

First, true joint custody—in the sense of sharing child care responsibility more or less equally—requires a number of unusual factors. Both parents must be capable and involved with the children. They must live close together so that travel between homes isn't too tiring. They must be able to afford two homes, each big enough to accommodate the children. (This alone eliminates most families.) They must communicate and resolve differences well, so that the children won't feel caught in the middle. Finally, the children themselves must be flexible enough to accept splitting their time between two different households.

Some people feel that it's best to have legal joint custody even if the parents won't really share child care responsibility. In fact, most legal joint custody arrangements involve a fairly traditional division of labor, with the mother taking day-to-day responsibility for the children.[10]

This idea has dangers of its own. The father still has an equal voice in all decisions, which the mother may then be left to implement. For example, the father could block a decision about where the mother and children would live, or he could insist that a child be allowed to engage in activities that the mother considers dangerous. If the parents can't agree, it will mean more trips back to court. If the father can afford to return to court but the mother can't, she might be forced to give in against her better judgment. She has the ultimate responsibility for child raising, but the father could get the practical power to make the major decisions.

Child support also may be reduced or eliminated, because the judge assumes that joint custody will mean equal responsibility (even when, in fact, it won't). Finally, joint custody is inappropriate where there is a history or danger of domestic violence, child sexual abuse, or kidnapping.

MYTH: Violence and abuse are not serious problems in the custody context. They don't happen often, and a concerned parent can always get protection when they do.

FACT: Violence and abuse are not uncommon problems, and protection can be difficult to obtain.

It is widely estimated that at least one husband in five is physically violent toward his wife.[11] Physical and sexual abuse of children is also shockingly common.[12] These problems don't go away just because the family separates, and they may get worse.

Despite these facts, judges sometimes fail to see or believe or protect against abuse. For example, some judges have awarded custody of children to men with an admitted history of alcoholism and wife beating, not realizing that these men are dangerous to children as well.[13] Some have awarded joint custody to men with an admitted history of child molestation (believing that the abuse would not continue), or awarded full custody despite evidence of child molestation (which the judge did not believe).[14] Although most judges will try to protect a child they truly believe is endangered, it's essential to document and prove fully the extent of the danger.

Even when abuse is documented, judges will generally permit an abusive father to visit the child. Concerned mothers must therefore be aware of procedures and options for protection.

MYTH: Custody is always decided legally.

FACT: Many fathers "win" custody, practically speaking, by illegally kidnapping their children from the mother. According to Richard Gelles, coauthor of *Behind Closed Doors: Violence in the American Family* (Doubleday Anchor, 1980), an estimated 459,000 to 751,000 parental kidnappings occur each year, and most of these are by fathers.[15]

Although parental kidnapping is clearly harmful and abusive to a child, not all fathers who kidnap children are consciously cruel or have abused their children in the past. This is because social attitudes that a man should be the "head of the household," combined with the traditional reluctance of law enforcement officials to interfere in "domestic disputes," have led some men to believe that paternal kidnapping is acceptable. Perhaps the worst example of this kind of thinking is that of a male lawyer who won custody of his own children and then, in a book urging other men to seek custody, devoted an entire chapter to suggested kidnapping techniques.[16]

MYTH: Men and women both have financial problems at divorce time, so finances don't affect their relative access to the legal system.

FACT: When the average couple with children divorce, their major family asset is the immediate earning power of the husband.[17] If the mother is caring for small children or has been out of the job market for some time, she may have no immediate earning power. The husband can go out and hire the best law firm in town to put on a stunning custody case, complete with expert witnesses and other proof. The wife, with limited funds, may have trouble finding even an adequate lawyer and pulling together a bare-bones case.

Additionally, financial factors can play a role in how the parents are perceived. A wealthy father may tell the judge he can offer the children a better home, a better neighborhood, a private school, a full-time housekeeper, and so on. Although there's no reason he couldn't achieve this by paying alimony or child support to the mother, many judges will nonetheless consider these direct advantages as factors favoring custody to the wealthier father.[18]

Indeed, many women are forced to give up custody of their children if they can't afford a court custody battle and/or they can't afford to raise the children alone. In an in-depth study of mothers who were involved in child custody disputes, reported in the book *Mothers on Trial* (McGraw-Hill, 1986), psychologist Phyllis Chesler found that severely lower incomes among the mothers were a major factor causing them to lose or give up custody. In fact, the greater the difference in earning power between mother and father, the more likely the mother was to lose custody. Sadly, these women had low incomes in large part *because* they had devoted themselves to caring for their children.[19]

MYTH: When women get custody (or even temporary custody) of the children, they also get the family home, and plenty of alimony and child support. After that, they won't have financial problems—the ex-husband who's supporting them will.

FACT: According to U.S. Census data for 1983, less than 5 percent of divorced or separated women raising children of the marriage were receiving any alimony.[20] Only 42 percent received any child support, and the average amount received by them was only about $125 per child per month.[21]

In fact, the leading study of the economic impact of divorce on men, women, and children shows that in the first year after divorce, the standard of living of the woman and any children plummets by an average 73 percent, while the man's standard of living actually *increases* by an average 42 percent.[22]

Additionally, a common pattern today is for the family home to be sold and the proceeds split in half between the parents.[23] Lenore Weitzman, the Stanford University sociologist who documented these postdivorce trends, explains: "It is at best only an *illusion* of equality. The man alone gets half the proceeds of the house, while the woman and two children must share the other half. Meanwhile, the family's most valuable asset—the earning power that the father built up over the years while the mother cared for the children— is barely shared at all."

Weitzman also found that men sometimes use threats to seek custody as a way of improving their bargaining position. Since many women will give up anything—the house, savings, even child support—to avoid custody loss, it is a disturbingly effective tool. Although, in Weitzman's study, only about one father in eight seriously sought custody, one in three used threats to seek custody as a tool in financial bargaining.[24]

MYTH: Only women who have been married to the child's father need to know about custody law and options.

FACT: Never-married women may have less reason for concern about an actual custody fight, because never-married men rarely seek custody of their children. But in most states, all fathers have the same basic legal rights regarding custody or visitation. (In actual practice, courts seem to be somewhat less receptive to a custody claim from a never-married father, but just as vigilant about his visitation rights.)

Because children usually do benefit from contact with both parents, a never-married mother may want to suggest a custody and visitation agreement even if the father doesn't. This is particularly so if the father has lived with the mother and child in the past.

Sometimes a never-married father seeks visitation with his child but is abusive. In that case, the mother may face the same difficulties in protecting her child that a mother who had been married to the father might.

MYTH: Custody is decided once. If a mother gets custody when the parents divorce, that's the end of that.

FACT: More than half of all custody disputes occur months or even years after divorce, when a noncustodial parent asks a court to modify the original custody order. The most common pattern appears to be that of a father who agrees when the parents divorce that the mother should have custody, but changes his mind when he remarries and/or he has objections to the mother's lifestyle or care of the children.[25]

Technically, judges are supposed to disfavor these modification actions, since a change of custody disturbs a child's stability. Yet in practice, the technical rules don't seem to have much effect.[26]

Sadly, a mother may be even *more* likely to lose custody when challenged after months or years of raising the children alone.[27] She's had time to make mistakes, as all active parents do—while the father, without the daily responsibility for child care, has had time to build his career, improve his standard of living, and possibly remarry. His lifestyle looks picture perfect, while hers is as realistically imperfect as any single parent's. Frequently, in that context, the mother's commitment to child raising is devalued.

THE POLITICS OF CHILD CUSTODY

How can this be? How can lawmakers and judges recognize the importance of stability, nurturance, and protection from physical and emotional harm in a child's life—and then follow policies that deprive countless children of precisely that security?

To understand the answer to that question, it's important to recognize a basic function of law in our society. The legal system acts to preserve social order. Frequently this is done by defending and protecting dominant social norms. Sometimes it is done by defending and protecting the rights of the powerful.

The two-parent family has always been a central social norm in our society. Divorce or family separation has been socially disfavored. However—perhaps because the lawmakers and judges have historically been men—the method chosen for discouraging divorce has always been to make it difficult and dangerous for *women* to leave marriages. In a sense, the men in power kept their freedom to come and go as they pleased, but made certain that they would not easily be left. The harm to children has been the sorry by-product of this effort to control women socially.

To understand the problem fully, it helps to know a little of its history. The ways of making it difficult for women to leave marriages have changed over time, but the basic theme is the same. It is also a history of society controlling women and children *within* marriages, even while preventing them from leaving. Ultimately, however, it is a picture of slow growth and progress toward healthier, more loving values.

Until about the early 1900s, married men legally had complete ownership of any property or savings their wives brought into the marriage, as well as any of their wives' earnings during the marriage.[28] Men also had the automatic legal right to the custody (and the wages) of their children. So if a woman dared to leave her husband—or even if he chose to evict her from the household—she would have to leave without the children (who could then be put to work), without property or savings, and often without any means of support.

That worked to keep women from leaving marriages, but it also rewarded men who exploited their wives and children. Thus, in the early 1900s, reformers were successful in passing new protective laws to curb the worst abuses. The Married Women's Property Acts established a woman's right to keep her own property and wages. Child labor laws protected children from economic exploitation, while child custody laws switched from granting fathers automatic custody to choosing on the basis of the best interests of children. In a minority of states, the law even officially favored the mother when deciding the custody of a very young child. (This reflected the social fact that women were the ones who cared for young children during marriage, so the child was protected from losing that relationship.)

It would be a mistake to think, however, that the reforms made it safe or even possible for women to leave their husbands or to live nontraditionally. In fact, until the recent advent of no-fault divorce, divorce wasn't even available as an option to most women.[29]

Technically, divorce was allowed for any man or woman who could prove serious fault (such as adultery or physical abuse) by the other spouse. But proving fault cost money for legal fees, detectives, medical reports, and so on. That meant that anyone lacking independent wealth (including lower-income men and nearly all women) couldn't, practically speaking, get a divorce that the other spouse opposed. For women raising children, there was also a serious risk of post-divorce poverty, since wage discrimination was severe, child support levels low, alimony uncommon, and support enforcement poor.

Basically, the only woman who could afford to get divorced was one who was without fault in causing the breakup (and perhaps still wanted to stay married), but who had a wealthy husband who very much wanted a divorce. In that case, the wife could bargain for child support and alimony, in return for her agreement not to oppose the divorce. A few very wealthy men paid quite a lot, giving rise to the old myths about ex-wives getting rich off their poor ex-husband's alimony checks. (In fact, few of the ex-husbands were poor, and not all the ex-wives were happy).

Interestingly, the trend in the 1970s toward no-fault divorce, now available in every state, was fueled both by advocates who wanted ordinary women to have the freedom to leave unhappy or abusive marriages, and by wealthy men who wanted the freedom to divorce more cheaply, without having to bargain for their wives' cooperation. Perhaps predictably, the result has been that both men and women can now get divorce on demand, but women and children are now even more likely to suffer postdivorce poverty.

Yet women, like men, keep divorcing. Even more alarming to many judges and legislators, some women seem to be making up new rules about how to live their lives, rather than living by the old rules. Today, outdated laws against sex outside marriage or sex with a same-sex partner are widely ignored, and old perceptions about "men's jobs" and "women's jobs" are slowly changing. More and more women are speaking their minds and making their own decisions.

Custody may be one of the last battlefields to try to keep women from living independent lives. Twenty years ago, the law would have made it very hard for you to get a divorce, and could have regulated your personal behavior after a divorce. Today, you can easily get a divorce—but you risk losing custody of your children if a judge finds your personal behavior objectionable.

It's no coincidence that many of the factors that judges use to determine custody are ones that favor the traditional "Father Knows Best" family. The remarried, career-oriented father with a stay-at-home wife is often favored over the working single mother. Certainly, any mother who strays from the traditional definition of a "good woman"—who is sexually active, politically outspoken, does not attend a church or synagogue, or is engaged in nontraditional work—has an increased risk of losing custody.

Ironically, you may consider yourself basically quite traditional, but still find that a judge thinks you're not traditional enough. You may have never wanted a divorce (but your husband insisted), and may hope to remarry (but haven't found a suitable partner). You may wish you could still live in the suburbs (but can't afford it), and may also wish you could stay home to care for your children daily (but need a full-time job so you all can eat). Yet there you are in the judge's eyes: a divorced, independent, citified career woman who never has time to bake brownies for the kids.

There have never been equal rights for divorcing women, or adequate protection for the children of divorce. Yet, like the slow, uneven advances in the law over time, there are some recent developments that can help. There is also a great deal that you can do to improve your chances and protect your children.

HOW TO USE THIS BOOK

The purpose of this book is to help you act rather than react in the custody context, whichever state you live in and whatever particular challenges you face. While you and your children face some real risks under our present system, there's no need to panic or despair. Like other dangers you face as a woman—wage discrimination, the threat of rape, or sexual harassment, to name a few—there are practical steps you can take to protect yourself and your children. By becoming informed about the problem and your options, you're already taking an important first step.

Keep in mind that a divorce or custody action is a lawsuit. The children's father has no legal duty to protect your rights or interests—or, for that matter, those of your mutual children. It is possible that he will take only actions calculated to help you and the children. It is also possible that, hurt and angry over the family breakup, he will try to use the law and even the children as weapons against you.

Most likely, his conduct will fall in between the two extremes. You may be able to gain his cooperation and goodwill in resolving custody decisions, but you can't assume that they will come easily. If you're concerned about what's right for both you and the children, you'll have to set goals and begin negotiating. Indeed, divorce and custody negotiation is a key first step in your new independent life.

Throughout this book, we'll focus on the concerns of women who have had the major (although not necessarily the exclusive) responsibility for child care, and who earn less money than the children's father. This is not to suggest that all families fit this pattern, and certainly doesn't reflect an idea that it should be that way. Realistically, however, it reflects the circumstances of *most* families and is a part of the difficulty that so many women face. That's why, without excluding other family types, we'll emphasize the more typical dilemmas.

You may be wondering, with the stress on possible custody conflicts, if this book is anti-father. Not at all. It is pro–involved parent. If a loving father has been involved in child raising in the past, it is absolutely in the child's best interests for that involvement to continue. If he has not been much involved in the past, but wants slowly to increase his role and responsibility with the child, that, too, is a healthy choice. That loving participation, however, is a far cry from an attempt to wrest custody away from the child's primary caretaker; or from the use of custody negotiations to show anger toward an ex-wife, express a preference for a new wife, gain a financial advantage, or express power and control. It is these latter abuses of custody law that you'll learn how to resist.

In fact, by learning how to resist possible abuse and intimidation, you open the door to a freer, more open development of a custody and visitation plan. Since, in most cases, it serves the children best to involve both parents, you'll be able to negotiate just that. The key element, however, is that you'll be more able to *act* in favor of the children's welfare instead of just *react* against threatened loss of custody.

It's a little bit like taking a self-defense course when you learn that women have been attacked on your street. You don't begin to walk down the street aiming karate chops at every passerby. Instead, you walk more calmly than you did before you took the course, because you now know that you can defend yourself if necessary. The danger is reduced, so you can better afford to smile at neighbors as you pass by.

Some people might argue, of course, that it's better not to know the dangers, because they'll only disturb your peace of mind. Yet when the stakes are so high, ignorance is *not* bliss. In Dr. Weitzman's study, one out of three women faced "custody blackmail" to reduce the already low standard of living they shared with their children. In Dr. Chesler's study, numerous women lost custody of—and some lost complete contact with—the children they had raised since birth. You can hope you'll never face any of these problems, and in fact you may not. But it's best to be prepared in case you do.

This book is designed to inform and support you as you consider each aspect of developing a custody plan. It applies if: (1) you are facing a possible divorce or separation now; (2) you want to defend your present custody arrangements against a possible challenge; or (3) you have lost custody and want the decision modified.

As you face these new challenges, it's essential to realize you're not alone. There are people who can help and work with you at every step of the process. In Chapter 2, we'll look at resources for emotional support and practical assistance for you and your children. In Chapter 3, we'll examine your options among lawyers and other professionals in the legal system. Since expenses are a real concern for most women, cost saving will be emphasized.

Most separating parents never go to court over custody or other divorce matters, but resolve their differences through negotiation. Therefore, in Chapter 4, we'll explore ways to develop a custody plan that truly serves the children's needs, with an emphasis on why continuity of care is so important. In Chapter 5, we'll work on developing a financial plan that can protect you and your children from poverty or financial loss.

The next task will be learning how to defend against possible dangers. Chapter 6 examines how traditional judgments about what constitutes "a good woman" can be used against you. Since custody disputes often center on these very judgments, you'll learn ways to guard against and offset them. Then, in Chapter 7 we'll examine how even the possibility of violence, sexual abuse, or paternal kidnapping can corrupt the custody process. For women whose children could be endangered, we'll explore specific protections available.

Unfortunately, negotiation doesn't always succeed. In Chapter 8, we'll look at your options when it does not. The custody investigation and hearing, the appeal process, and custody modification actions are all discussed. Chapter 9 is devoted to the process of healing and looking toward the future.

Being a mother is challenging, and divorce or separation today adds a whole new set of challenges. Yet you've met the first challenge, and you'll learn to meet the others. You'll find you need to work and plan and advocate on your children's behalf, but also that you have strengths you never realized you had. With time, your hard work will show itself in a re-structured, healthy, peaceful family life. That alone is im-portant hope for the future.

2 | GATHERING YOUR STRENGTH

Family separation is difficult and painful. With children, it's even tougher. You're upset and so are they, but you're supposed to be the strong one. And just as it seems your whole world is falling apart, you are thrust into key negotiations affecting how you and the children will live for the next several years.

Before you begin planning your independent future, it makes sense to be sure you've fully explored your options within the marriage. Divorce is more painful than most people expect, and there are at least some divorced parents who now wish they could turn the clock back.

Consider, for example, the case of Marilyn and Doug Clark.° Marilyn asked for a divorce largely because Doug seemed uninterested in family life and often worked or watched television all weekend. She was frustrated and unhappy enough to see divorce as the solution, but she also secretly hoped her request would shock Doug into changing his ways. It did, but not quite as she'd hoped.

Doug moved out of the house angrily, too hurt even to discuss the future. Communicating through lawyers, the two agreed on custody of their two young sons (in Marilyn), weekend visitation, and modest support. Yet Marilyn was amazed to watch Doug become an active and involved weekend parent. The simple truth was that divorce made Doug reevaluate his priorities, and he realized that family life really was important to him. He couldn't just take his children for

° Like all examples in this book, the names have been changed but the story is real. In some cases, a profile is based on several similar cases.

granted now that seeing them meant planning and effort. Eventually Doug remarried and fathered another child, this time as a more active partner with the mother.

Marilyn doesn't miss the old Doug, but sometimes she's wistful that she never got to enjoy the new Doug. The boys, now teenagers, have adjusted well, but they, too, feel a sad sense of loss.

Divorce is a time of crisis and challenge, and many men and women experience enormous personal growth in its wake. Ironically, sometimes the changes are precisely those that would have made the marriage stronger. That's why it's worth it for couples considering divorce to ask not only "Can this marriage work?" but "Can we change and grow to make this marriage work?"

Sometimes, too, the urge to divorce isn't really caused by problems within the marriage so much as by other life crises. When a child dies, for example, the parents are very likely to divorce soon after, even if they considered the marriage happy before the death. Anxiety over reaching middle age is another common catalyst to divorce. Divorce can be a way of running away from a problem instead of working through painful feelings. Unfortunately, the divorce can create new problems without ever solving the old ones.

If you're not separated now, but are just thinking about divorce, you might want to explore marriage counseling or family therapy first. If you're separated but starting to consider reconciliation, it's worth it to say so directly to your husband. Occasionally both partners secretly want to get back together but are too proud to admit it.

Yet if you've decided that divorce is really the best alternative, have had that decision announced to you by your spouse, or even if you are simply exploring your options, you're wise to look ahead. Divorce can be a strengthening experience as well as a difficult one. Planning about custody and care of the children in particular will be key to making the transition as healthy and positive as possible.

Be aware that it's normal to feel a great deal of stress and depression for the first several months of separation.

You're ending a major part of your life. A marriage you had hoped was made in heaven is now being settled in court.

It's also normal for your children to be unhappy now. Their lives are being disrupted, and they may respond with sadness, anger, confusion, or misbehavior. They may act rather unlovable—but actually be crying out for your continued love and reassurance.

Eventually, most of the turmoil will pass. Both adults and children have an amazing ability to bounce back, and even to emerge stronger, from a crisis.

What will remain, of course, are the terms of your custody, support, and property agreement. If they are realistic and positive, they'll help speed the healing process. If they're punitive or disruptive, the pain and family instability will continue.

Fortunately, negotiating a positive agreement about custody and related financial matters doesn't mean ignoring your personal needs and focusing only on the legal process. Quite the contrary. If you can reach out for help and support from friends, family, and others, you will both feel better *and* be better able to negotiate from a position of strength. Similarly, if you pay some attention to your own emotional needs, you'll have more to give to your children. You'll also project a stronger, more stable image as your children's caretaker, which will be helpful in custody negotiations.

There are other, very practical concerns that will need your attention, both in their own right and to prepare you for custody negotiations. Budgeting, career, child care, and perhaps housing may all be areas of your life needing new energy and attention. Again, the more planning and networking you can do, the better prepared you'll be.

This chapter is about marshaling your resources to meet your own pressing emotional and practical needs, while also helping your children with their needs. This is important, for both personal and practical reasons. Often, divorcing spouses encounter extra difficulties if they jump into the legal process without getting some emotional support first. All kinds of feelings get mixed up in the negotiations: anger, guilt, fear of independence, even fear of renewed closeness with the ex-spouse. That can lead to more difficult negotiations, higher legal fees, impractical agreements—and still no relief for the underlying feelings.

There are also a number of coping strategies you'll want to avoid. Some people, for example, are so shaken by a divorce that they look to their lawyers to "save" them. Their lawyers don't save them—in fact, faced with a passive, uninvolved client, it's difficult for a lawyer to do even an adequate job. Again, the legal case suffers while the underlying problem is ignored or even worsened.

An equally tempting—and equally self-defeating—coping mechanism is to run out and find a new lover to save you. First of all, it's a terrible way to begin a new relationship, and you might end up with more problems than you had in the marriage you're leaving. Further, it could spell trouble in case of a custody dispute if you are reinvolved before the divorce is final. Even if you're separated, a not-yet-divorced woman with a lover is considered an adulteress. There are still plenty of judges who take that as a sign of unfitness—whether or not the husband has similarly strayed. Unfortunately, the double standard is alive and well in many courts to this day.

Finally, another very understandable, very problematic way of dealing with stress and loneliness is to turn to your children for help and comfort. Even if they seem to understand and want to hear your troubles, it's extremely hard on them. Knowing how worried you are, they're certain to feel more anxious at an already difficult time. And since so much of your sadness and anger revolves around their father, they'll feel helplessly caught in the middle. If for no other reason than to spare your children the burden of your anxiety, it's best to find other sources of help and support.

As you read through the suggestions that follow, use your imagination. Think creatively about the resources in your own community and the needs in your life. Every time you find yourself thinking "I can't afford that" or "I don't have time," take a minute to explore whether there are free or low-cost services available, or whether it's important enough for you to make time. While it's true that you're likely to be both limited in time and short of funds during the divorce process, it's also true that it's often difficult to ask for help. Sometimes there's a natural temptation to make excuses rather than admit one's needs.

This is one time in your life when it makes sense to set aside any false pride. You deserve and have a right to take care of yourself and your children. If that means searching out resources for help and support, it's a good and healthy choice.

EMOTIONAL SUPPORT

For many women, *friends or family members* provide a crucial supportive role in dealing with the emotional stress of separation and single parenting. You may have a history of closeness and trust with an old friend, and that can help you to be open now. Friends are also available immediately and don't cost money. It's comforting, too, just to be around people who love and understand you, who know you've been happy before and will be so again.

Yet there are drawbacks to choosing old friends and family members as your only or primary confidants. Often, despite their desire to help, they have conflicting feelings of their own. If your mother is upset by seeing you sad, she may urge you to cheer up just when you need most to cry. If your brother always liked your husband and felt they had a lot in common, it may be hard for him to hear about your anger. If your best friend closely identifies with you and fears her own marriage may be in trouble, the whole subject of your divorce may feel threatening to her. None of these reactions (or other nervous responses you may encounter) is a rejection of you, but each does limit how helpful a confidant that friend can be.

Choosing old friends as primary confidants can also put them in the middle. Just as it hurts children to hear about anger toward their other parent, mutual friends can also become uncomfortable. They may feel forced to choose sides or even to abandon their closeness with both of you.

Old friends and family members could also be required to testify in court if there's eventually a dispute over custody. That could create a problem if you'd chosen them to hear all your deepest fears and doubts. For example, suppose that, in the midst of crying, you told a friend, "Oh, sometimes I wish I could just sleep forever." That's natural enough as a short-term response to extreme stress, and usually reflects a wish for peace more than a wish to die. Yet repeated in court, it could sound suicidal, raising questions over stability and fitness for child raising.

Note that a friend or family member may not legally refuse to testify in court. If you'd confided in your personal therapist, however, the therapist wouldn't be allowed to testify in most states unless you gave permission. The same is true of your priest, rabbi, or minister. Other confidants you might choose, such as a counselor on a crisis hot line or a member of an anonymous self-help group, would probably never be identified as potential witnesses.

Finally, your friends simply aren't trained to help you deal with a severe life crisis, and they may not have had similar experiences which could help them to understand. That's why it's often wise to look for others, with either training or personal experience to help you.

Yet while it's good to be realistic about your friends' limitations, there's certainly no need to shut yourself off from them. To the contrary, you need your friends now more than ever. It's fine to be honest about ordinary feelings of sadness; that's quite different from depending on your friends as your only emotional outlet. Friends and family are also a wonderful resource for cheering up and getting away, for help in child care and organizing, and for just plain helping you feel lovable again.

Who can help when you need emotional support you can't get from your friends? *Self-help support groups* are a wonderful resource that, like friends, don't charge for services. Their special strength is that they can provide a nurturing community of people who understand just what you're going through because they've been there themselves. You'll realize that you're not alone, that your feelings are absolutely normal, and that things will get better. As you hear how other people solve problems similar to your own, you'll pick up new ideas and inspiration. You may also be surprised to find other people learning from *your* ideas, which is a great way to discover you're stronger and smarter than you knew.

Self-help groups vary in focus, and you'll want to give some thought to which are right for you. Some are a lot like group therapy, minus the therapist: They're a safe place to cry or rage and receive comfort from other members. Others (discussed later in this chapter) are more like social groups for members with a common interest, or focus on practical needs like court preparation or job planning. Although some groups require a short-term time commitment, most operate on a "come when you need it" basis. Almost all self-help groups are completely confidential, but to be sure, you can ask about group policies.

Local self-help groups may be listed in the phone book, in your local newspaper's community events column, or with a telephone hot line for community services. Groups with national offices appear in Appendix C of this book, and the central office can put you in touch with local groups.

The most obvious choice among self-help groups would be a support group for people going through divorce. If you have a choice, you might want to give serious thought to a mixed group of women and men rather than an all-women's group. While some divorce-related problems (such as finances and child raising) are generally worse for women, the central problems of loss and loneliness are common to everyone. You might find it a comfort, particularly if you hope someday to have a male partner again, to be reminded that in inner feelings at least, men and women are more similar than different.

But a word to the wise: Therapy-type support groups of any kind are a terrible place to look for a new partner, even once you're divorced. It's too easy for the new relationship to get dragged down in old sorrows, and any in-group dating can ruin your feeling of safety within the group. Yet the sense of closeness that develops as group members share their feelings (combined with loneliness) can make sexual involvement a real temptation. Some women choose all-women's groups simply to avoid that kind of conflict. Others choose women's groups to help themselves avoid too much dependence on men to "solve their problems."

Family separation may also be a time to heal old wounds or build new strengths. Help is available, again through community resources or referral services listed in Appendix C. Consider:

- Single-parent support groups or parent-child support groups can be an important part of coping with new demands on you and your children.
- If you have trouble controlling your anger with your children, Parents Anonymous is an excellent resource, using a combined self-help and volunteer professional leader format.
- If your husband is or was a heavy drinker, his drinking had to affect you and all the family relationships. Al-Anon Family Groups can help you to regain your own peace of mind, and also offers Ala-Teen support groups for teens (twelve and up) and preteens (eight to eleven).
- You can also get help if you're concerned about your own drinking (or want to learn more about problem drinkers). Alcoholics Anonymous has "open" meetings for anyone who wants to learn about alcoholism, as well as confidential "closed" meetings for people concerned about their own drinking.
- If you are afraid of your husband or were physically or sexually abused during the marriage, a support group for formerly battered women may be an important part of rebuilding your self-esteem and protecting your own and your children's safety.
- If you think that problems you're having now in your marriage or in parenting are related to growing up in an alcoholic home, you might at some point want to

attend an Adult Children of Alcoholics support group available through Al-Anon Family Groups. Similarly, if you were sexually abused as a child, you might want to attend an Incest Survivors group. (Divorce helps—or sometimes forces—many women to examine their own family lives as children. Many, however, find it's best to wait until the immediate crisis is past before beginning to explore old feelings.)

Some divorcing parents find help from *religious leaders* with training or experience in pastoral counseling. If you have a minister or rabbi you especially trust and respect, this may be an option for you. You should be aware, though, that some religious leaders are oriented toward helping partners to reconcile. That's good if reconciliation is still a possibility, but if the marriage is truly over, you could find yourself at cross-purposes with such a counselor. Also, most clergy members are middle-aged men, and some have very traditional views of a wife's duty to her husband. That may be the last thing you need to hear just as you're struggling to create a healthy independent life for yourself and your children.

If you're looking for emotional support in a religious setting, there may be other options open to you. Divorced Catholics groups are active in many communities, and some Protestant and Jewish groups also exist. In urban areas, women's theological groups or even nonreligious women's centers may help you to find clergywomen of your faith.

A final important source of emotional support and rebuilding is *professional therapists*. If you have health insurance or belong to a health maintenance organization (HMO), the services you need may be covered. Be sure to check policy terms carefully, because coverage varies according to the type of therapist (such as psychiatrist, psychologist, or social worker), the type of therapy (individual, group, or family), and how long you use the services. Many community health centers or mental health centers offer services on a sliding scale. It pays to shop around, both for price and for a program that's right for you.

Individual therapy can be a very good choice, particularly if you're suffering from serious depression or other major stress reactions. It can offer the safety of a confidential meeting with a person specially trained to help people in crisis.

Group therapy can provide the advantages of sharing feelings and ideas as in self-help support groups, but in a more structured and directed setting. Just as in the self-help groups, therapy groups are often structured to meet specific needs, such as those of single or divorcing parents.

Family therapy isn't just for spouses who hope to reconcile. It can be extremely helpful in making the transition to a new, separated family. Family members (including children) can work through feelings of anger, sadness, and loss, and begin to learn ways to cooperate in the newly divided family structure.

This is very important to women when we consider all the opportunities men have in the current legal system to express their feelings in a negative, even destructive way. Therapy—individual or family—can provide a far more positive outlet. Although many divorcing men refuse individual therapy because they don't want to seem "weak" or "weird," those same men may agree to the more goal-directed family separation therapy. For the many basically caring men who really want to resolve their feelings, but who could easily be sidetracked into power and control maneuvers, family counseling can provide an excellent alternative.

(It should be noted that in extreme cases such as battering or sexual abuse, counseling alone won't remove the need for legal protections. Indeed, counseling without legal protection could be counterproductive, because it could create the impression that violence and abuse are negotiable issues. "Okay, I'll quit hitting you if you'll quit bugging me about how I treat the kids" is not an acceptable offer. Similarly, tears shed in therapy over abusing a child are no substitute for stopping the abuse. For more on stopping violence and abuse, see Chapter 7.)

A final form of therapy to consider is parent-child therapy. Family separation is a difficult time for children, and can damage their trust in both parents. Even if the father leaves and the mother retains custody, the mother-child relationship often suffers. Additionally, your own pain and the new responsibilities of single parenthood can create a serious strain. Mother-child therapy can help mend any breaches and form a stronger bond. That's important in its own right, and is doubly important if you anticipate custody conflicts.

Note that it's quite possible to use a mixed approach, with more than one type of therapy or support group. For example, you could begin individual therapy during the worst of the divorce crisis, then switch to group therapy or a divorce self-help group when you were feeling stronger (or perhaps when your insurance coverage ended). You could meet with a therapist who sometimes saw you alone, sometimes saw you with your child, and sometimes saw your child alone. But any therapist who sees you and your husband together over a period of time shouldn't double as your or his personal therapist. In that case, it's better to have the roles clear.

In choosing a therapist, start with a referral from a reputable agency to a licensed professional. If you're interested in family or child therapy, make sure the therapist is trained and experienced in that area. Then trust your instincts when you meet. There should be a feeling of rapport: of respect, but also of trust. You don't want someone who intimidates you, but neither are you looking for a buddy.

For an individual therapist, strongly consider a woman. Too many women go from depending on a father to depending on a husband to depending on a father/husband–figure therapist. Additionally, a minority of male therapists take sexual advantage of distraught female clients. While most do not, why take an unnecessary risk?

As for what kind of therapist, the most common choices are an MSW (with a master's degree in social work, and a specialty in counseling) or a psychologist (with a master's or Ph.D. in clinical psychology). Generally speaking, an MSW is more oriented toward family and group dynamics, while a psychologist is trained to dig a little deeper into an individual's feelings and coping mechanisms. Either can be an excellent choice.

It is usually not best to choose a psychiatrist unless you need a specialist, or a psychiatrist is specifically recommended by a psychologist or an MSW. Even then, you might want to get a second opinion. Psychiatrists are medical doctors with advanced training in psychiatry, and they are generally more expensive than other therapists. Also, because psychiatrists often see seriously troubled clients, they may tend to label all clients unnecessarily.

For example, it's normal when getting a divorce to feel energized and independent at times, depressed and lonely at other times. Yet some psychiatrists might call those mood swings "manic depressive." Later, if you went to court over a custody problem, the very fact that you were seeing a psychiatrist could make the judge wonder if you were having serious emotional problems. (This may not be fair, but it's common.) If you agreed to have the psychiatrist testify, only to have him (most psychiatrists are men) describe you as manic depressive, that could make things worse.

Incidentally, it's worth commenting on the tendency for judges and others to wonder about the mental health of someone seeing a psychiatrist. For the most part, the same thing does not happen if you're getting help from a psychologist, an MSW, a pastoral counselor, or a self-help group. Most judges realize that divorce creates a serious life stress and respect those who get help in dealing with it. More important, they'll see the results in your greater peace of mind and strengthened relationships with your children.

If you live in a very rural area, however, old prejudices about mental health professionals may persist. This shouldn't keep you from getting the help you need, but it could affect where you turn for help. In case of doubt, discuss the question with your attorney as soon as possible.

MEETING PRACTICAL NEEDS

You'll need other practical resources in planning a new life. There are a number of free or low-cost groups that can be a big help. None are an alternative to a lawyer, but they can help you to work more productively with your lawyer. In many cases, they'll fill needs that are not addressed by lawyers.

If you've been away from the paid workforce for a while, you'll need job-search planning and perhaps job training or education. Many communities offer *displaced homemaker programs,* often through local women's centers. They can help you to develop and market your skills, make arrangements for child care, and find training and education resources. Most of these services are low-cost.

Women's centers, particularly those with emergency shelters for women and children in crisis, may be able to help you with a variety of practical needs for little or no charge. If you'll need new housing, a new job, or a child care center, for example, a women's center may be able to put you in touch with local resources.

Parents Without Partners, also listed in Appendix C, is a resource many divorcing women and men find rewarding. Primarily it's a social group, a way of making new friends who share your concerns as a single parent. (It may also be a heavy dating scene, so be forewarned if you're not divorced or not looking.) But PWP has also moved beyond its singles club roots, and many chapters offer educational programs, child care resources, and discussion groups.

If you think you may have to face a serious custody conflict, you'll need lots of emotional support, as well as practical help in dealing with the legal system. Perhaps the most helpful resource available is a group originally formed to provide mutual support for mothers who have lost custody, but which has expanded its focus to include women facing current custody disputes.

Now known as Mothers Without Custody (they may change their name to reflect the wider focus), the group began when a Massachusetts talk show host began to speak on the air about the loss of her child's custody. Other mothers who had faced a similar loss contacted her, and they decided to join together for mutual support. They have grown to a national network of local groups (listed in Appendix C) and provide practical and emotional support to any woman affected by a custody dispute. They particularly stress options for mother/child involvement (whatever the eventual custody ruling) and provide education programs whenever possible.

If there is no Mothers Without Custody group active near you, the national office will still help you to get in touch with other women who share your concerns. You may also want to check with another national network known as The Child Support Network (see Appendix C). Similar in organization to Mothers Without Custody, these are grassroots groups of parents (mostly mothers) who have had difficulty collecting child support for their children. Although their emphasis may be slightly different from your own, you'll find that many groups offer helpful experience and savvy with the legal system.

Some groups, for example, offer "mock trials" so you can practice testifying about your case. Since child support and custody problems are often related, some group members may have experienced custody disputes as well. At the very least, you will find group members understanding and supportive as you face new challenges.

However alone you feel now, you can see that there are people who can help and support you during this difficult time. By reaching out for help and information now, you're taking a responsible step toward a better future for yourself and your children.

3 ☐ WORKING WITHIN THE LEGAL SYSTEM

Not every legal task requires a lawyer. Without a lawyer, you can sue in small claims court or defend yourself against a minor traffic charge. For an uncomplicated child support collection case, you might be able to get adequate help from a government collection service. But for any case involving child custody questions, you absolutely, positively must have a lawyer—and as good a one as possible. Too much is at stake for you to take unnecessary risks.

CHOOSING A LAWYER

Ideally, choosing a lawyer shouldn't be too rushed. Your choice of attorney is an important factor in resolving your case well. Some careful comparison shopping now can save you endless headaches later.

Sometimes, of course, there's no time to choose slowly and carefully. If your first knowledge of the coming divorce is learning that your husband has withdrawn all your joint savings and rented a moving van, you need a lawyer today. In that case, you might consider a time-limited arrangement with any reputable attorney experienced in family law. For example: "I'll pay you two hundred dollars to seek a court order immediately to stop my husband from leaving with our money and property. Next week, we'll talk about whether you should handle the entire custody and support action."

In most cases, however, it doesn't hurt to take a week or two to choose an attorney. Certainly, it's better to put in the initial work of finding a good lawyer than to be stuck in midstream with a poor one. While it's possible to switch later, it's often expensive and disruptive. And there's no need to panic if you're contacted by your husband's lawyer. Simply send a brief letter saying you are not yet represented by a lawyer but are looking for one.

According to William Bolger, executive director of the National Resource Center for Consumers of Legal Services, finding a good lawyer is a lot like finding a good restaurant. Your best bet is to begin by asking for suggestions among people whose judgment you trust and whose circumstances are similar to your own. Thus, if you have friends who've been divorced, you could start by asking if their lawyers were helpful. Begin a list of possible choices, with these names at the top.

Another good resource is referrals from local women's centers or battered-women's shelters (even if you don't have a violence problem). Make sure the recommendation really means: "We know this person does good divorce and custody work," and not: "This is a wonderful person who's politically active on important causes." Similarly, if you have any friends who are lawyers—even business or real estate lawyers—ask who's known in the legal community as a good domestic (family law) attorney. You might also ask who's awful and should be avoided.

In many communities, family lawyers regularly speak at open meetings in churches and libraries on topics related to divorce. It's a way of attracting clients; you can use it to get free information *and* size up a possible lawyer for yourself. Check for such speakers in your local newspaper or with other community resources.

As a last resort, you can gather names of lawyers who handle family law cases by contacting your state or local bar association. Inquire if they list lawyers by specialty areas and how much experience is required to be listed. You might also ask for the names of the officers of the family law sections of the state and local bar, as well as the officers of the local women's bar association.

Finally, check with the bar association to see if any of the lawyers you've listed (from all sources) have had disciplinary actions against them. Strike any who have from your list.

Your next step is to begin calling the lawyers' offices. Over the phone, ask about costs, experience, and type of practice. This will help you decide whom you want to meet in person. Since many lawyers do not charge (or charge only a modest fee) for a first visit, you may be able to meet several before making a final choice.

Your first appointment will be a two-way interview. You'll be evaluating the lawyer, and he or she will be evaluating your case. Organize your information before you come and expect to answer questions—but don't be shy about asking your own questions.

If you feel uncomfortable or intimidated, trust your instincts. That's probably a sign that this isn't the lawyer for you. You deserve courtesy, clear explanations, and an atmosphere of mutual trust and respect. If you don't get them, try elsewhere.

If your case has special features, you'll want to ask over the phone about the lawyer's experience with those specific problems. A case involving possible hidden income or assets, for example, would require a lawyer with substantial background in evaluating business and financial records. If you think there might be a custody fight, you'll need a lawyer who has successfully represented women challenged for custody. Some lawyers are experienced in both, which is a definite plus.

NEGOTIATION STYLES

There are two extreme types among lawyers that can seem good but actually spell trouble. One is the high-powered litigator known as a "bomber." This lawyer, while often very knowledgeable and persuasive, is much more skilled at competing than at cooperating. Although a dangerous enemy for your husband in the courtroom, the bomber may be more likely than a low-key lawyer to unnecessarily force the case into court in the first place.

For example, if your husband is now somewhat hurt and angry, an assertive but nonthreatening lawyer might still be able to work out a compromise. A bomber, on the other hand, could easily provoke that anger into rage—and then "heroically" defend you against the rage. That heroic defense might mean an all-out court fight, uproar in the family for years, and sky-high attorney fees.

At the other extreme is the lawyer who is wonderfully sensitive and compassionate, but who lacks the assertiveness to bargain effectively. This is someone who might be a wonderful, comforting friend during a divorce, but is expensive—perhaps even dangerous—as your lawyer. You may have to insist on arrangements your husband doesn't particularly like, and you need a lawyer who's not too polite to disagree with your husband's attorney.

Note that these two extremes are the same as extremes of stereotypical male and female behavior: male aggressiveness and female passivity. Not surprisingly (and despite exceptions), the bomber style tends to be more common among male lawyers, while the "too nice" approach is a risk with some women lawyers.

The best lawyers are those—female or male—who combine the best of traditionally male and traditionally female traits. They are assertive but able to cooperate, understanding but businesslike, fair but firm. They will vigorously protect your legal rights and promote your best interests, but will not stir up trouble with lavish promises of what they "can get you" in court.

Of course, there's not one large set of perfect lawyers smack in between bombers and too nice lawyers. There's a whole spectrum, with some individuals especially strong in asserting your rights, while others are especially talented at gaining the other side's cooperation. (Then again, some lawyers are talented at nothing, but no one has to tell you to weed them out.)

If you're considering a lawyer who seems capable and conscientious, try to get a picture of where she or he fits on the assertiveness spectrum. Then think about your own needs.

If your husband is abusive or seems determined to fight a power battle, you may need a somewhat more aggressive lawyer to protect your rights. On the other hand, maybe you know from experience that you and your husband solve problems best when you can both calm down and work out a compromise. In that case, it would probably help to look for a lawyer who is more attuned to a cooperative approach.

The best lawyer of all is one flexible enough to let the other side set the tone. Your lawyer should be willing to tell your husband's lawyer, "Look, we want to settle this amicably and we're ready to do so. But if you and your client want to fight, we're ready for that too. I'll defend my client's rights vigorously, by every legal means available."

AFFORDING LEGAL COSTS

For many women, the first stumbling block toward getting a good lawyer is money. Very few lawyers will handle a divorce or custody case without at least some cash up front. Before you despair, however, realize that there are a lot of lawyers today and they need your business. With persistence and perhaps some negotiating of your own, you should be able to work out payment arrangements if your cash is limited.

Most lawyers will, if necessary, agree to installment payments and/or put off collecting the major portion of the legal fee until after property and support are settled. If nothing else, your lawyer should agree to negotiate for a temporary order of custody, child support, and, if possible, alimony before expecting full payment. If you have a joint checking or savings account, that should also be considered as a possible source of immediate funds. Talk this over with your lawyer *right away* (over the phone if necessary), before that joint account mysteriously disappears.

Your lawyer and your husband's lawyer may suggest a final divorce agreement that allows them to collect their legal fees directly from the property being divided. Another possibility is your husband's agreeing, as part of the financial negotiations, to pay a sum for attorney fees to your lawyer.

Or, after it's all over, your lawyer could ask the judge to order your husband to pay part of your attorney fees. All these can be reasonable solutions—so long as you don't depend on them in advance. If your lawyer thinks that he or she won't be paid reliably by you but needs to look to your husband for payment, there's a temptation to please your husband instead of you. That could hurt your case. For that reason, plan clearly how you'll pay attorney fees—and be pleasantly surprised if your husband is later ordered to help.

Also keep in mind that money that comes from the marital property or from your husband's income is not free. It means less money to divide and less that could go to support the children. That's why this money, too, should be reasonably limited to fair payment for necessary legal services.

The more you take the initiative in setting up a payment plan, the more likely you are to have it accepted. For example, you could say, "I can't pay two thousand dollars now, but I can pay five hundred out of the joint savings and one hundred a month for a year. That's seventeen hundred, and perhaps we could talk about ways to cut costs to make up the difference." That's more likely to win you agreement than: "Gosh, two thousand dollars! Can I pay you after I'm back on my feet financially?"

Try to be realistic about what you'll be able to pay and then stick to the plan. You may need your lawyer again later, and it won't help if you're behind in your payments. If a lawyer you're considering won't offer a reasonable payment plan, keep looking until you find one who will.

It's essential that you get in writing a clear agreement regarding:

- What you will be required to pay in attorney fees.
- What other court costs are expected.
- When you'll have to pay, and in what installments.
- What efforts the attorney will make to collect instead from the marital property or from the children's father (including appropriate limits).

- Exactly what services you'll be getting for your money.

The last point may be the most important of all: What services will you get for your money? Probably the commonest complaint about a divorce lawyer is: "He took my money and disappeared"—not to Mexico, but to an overcrowded schedule. A woman may pay a lawyer a set fee (often all she has) for what she thinks is the whole case, only to learn that the lawyer plans to charge more after the initial negotiations. Sometimes this is due to honest misunderstanding. In other cases, the lawyer is taking advantage of the woman's confusion and distress. There is only one way to minimize the risk: *Get it in writing.* If a problem develops later, make it clear that you are willing to complain to the state disciplinary board if necessary.

It's possible that you simply don't have the money to pay for the legal services you need, even with a payment plan, and don't know when you will. Or you may need immediate funds for other court-related costs, such as the deposition of an expert witness (see Chapter 8). This can happen particularly in a prolonged custody battle, where the legal fees keep mounting long after the property is divided or spent on legal costs. If you're disabled or unemployed, it can be even worse.

There are no easy solutions, but some women show enormous resourcefulness. Some explain to parents or other relatives the seriousness of the problem and ask for help with a portion of the costs. Some borrow from friends. One woman knew her family and friends had no money to spare, so she asked them instead if they could donate to a large yard sale. Another woman, already active in a women's center, received fund-raising help from them. Other women, in cities with good public transportation, have sold their car. None of these are easy solutions, but they may be the best in a bad situation.

If you have a close friend who wants to help, you might ask her to organize some fund-raising for you. Bake sales, car washes, yard sales, or even a benefit concert are just a few ideas. Obviously, you'll want to protect your family's privacy, though, in publicizing any events.

Another option to investigate is free legal assistance from your local Legal Services Corporation office. In many areas, these programs offer excellent services—if you can get them to take your case. Legal Services lawyers tend to be hard-working, idealistic young attorneys, swamped by too many cases and too little funding. In fact, because of recent federal funding cuts, most programs have been cut back severely. Commonly, family law programs have been the first to go.

By all means check your local Legal Services program, because offices vary in what they'll offer. Some have responded to the cuts by handling only the simplest cases: uncontested divorces where there's no dispute over custody and little money to divide. Others handle only the most serious cases, such as those involving a threat of violence or an incestuous father who wants custody or overnight visitation.

If your case does involve a threat of violence or incest, be sure to mention it over the phone. Otherwise, you might be put on a low-priority waiting list when you need services right now.

If you are offered a space on a waiting list, first make certain that you're definitely eligible for services and ask how long a wait is expected, and what services will be offered when your name comes up. There's no point in waiting a year to have a lawyer tell you the organization doesn't handle cases like yours.

Clearly, your goal in looking for a lawyer is to find the best one you can afford. Fortunately, best doesn't always mean most expensive. Although it's generally true that more experienced lawyers charge more, there's a great deal of variation in individual talent and knowledge. Also, a good lawyer doesn't exist in a vacuum; the best lawyer may be the one who works best with you.

WORKING WITH YOUR LAWYER

The most talented lawyer in the world can't resolve your custody case effectively unless you're actively involved. You need to be ready to do some footwork, assist in planning, prod when necessary, and make major decisions.

Keep in mind that a lawyer has many cases. You have one: yours. Naturally, you'll be putting more energy and thought into that one crucial case. Most important, you and your children are the ones who will live with whatever custody arrangements are negotiated.

Whenever you meet with your lawyer, arrive on time, prepared with information about recent family developments, any forms you've been asked to prepare, and a list of your own questions. That will help speed up your case and save interview time for more in-depth strategizing.

You'll work best with your lawyer if you work cooperatively, trading ideas and information. As you read this book, you'll learn a lot about making a strong case, and will probably have both questions and ideas. By all means share them. The best lawyers learn not only from lawbooks but from their clients as well.

As the case progresses, stay in close contact. While you should avoid unnecessary calls, it's fine to call to ask about delays or to supply new information. The open lines of communication will help your lawyer to stay informed about your case, and may keep you from being lost in the shuffle.

If you don't get the service and commitment your case deserves, there are remedies available to you. You could switch lawyers. You could complain to your state disciplinary board. Yet, if possible, it's best to keep these as last resorts and try to work out the problem with the lawyer first.

HOW TO NEED YOUR LAWYER LESS

There's a great deal that you can do in your private life to help make your case go smoothly. As much as possible, avoid unnecessary arguments with the children's father. They can heighten any hostility, strain family relations, and even hurt your custody case. It's natural to be angry during a divorce or separation, but you'll be better off if you put your energies into planning your own life and enjoying your children. If your husband tries to start an argument, back off if you can.

It may come as a surprise to you, but far more divorce and custody cases are resolved by agreement than are ever solved by a judge. In fact, at least 90 percent of all divorces are settled by the parties and never go to court at all. You can be sure that many of those cases started with both spouses angry and unwilling to agree, but the fact remains that less than one in ten actually persists to trial.

For bargaining reasons, though, you have to be prepared to go to trial if necessary—or at least *look* willing to do so. Clearly, there are many reasons to want to avoid a trial: It's unpleasant, it's expensive, and it can upset the children. Yet the minute you tell your husband, "I'd never go through a court trial," you've lost your bargaining power. He and his lawyer know they can make all kinds of unreasonable demands because you won't go to court to defend your rights.

The key to getting results in the ordinary case is to be fair but firm. Insist upon your rights and upon what you feel is best for the children, but treat the children's father with courtesy and respect. You should also keep in mind the importance of obeying court orders, whether or not the children's father does the same. Court orders are like laws; it can be dangerous to break them. In some cases, it's even more dangerous for a custodial mother to do so.

For example, if the children's father got mad and refused to pay support for a few months, he might face a reprimand, the collection of support from his paycheck, or even (unlikely) a night in jail. But if you got mad and prevented court-ordered visitation between father and child, you could risk losing custody in many states. That's obviously a risk you don't want to take.

Fortunately, you'll be less tempted to violate any agreement that you were actively involved in planning. Even if you don't agree with every provision—even if you think much of it is somewhat unwise or unfair—you'll have the satisfaction of knowing you were informed and consulted in structuring the basic agreement. That, more than anything else, is the best argument for working closely and cooperatively with your lawyer.

THE MEDIATION OPTION

Some divorcing or separating couples find divorce mediation helpful in resolving conflicts. There are private mediation services in many communities, and some court systems offer free mediation services.

Although family law mediation has some good points, it also can present some very real dangers. Before you agree to mediation, you should be sure you understand exactly what it is and how it can affect your case.

Mediation involves two or more people with a legal or personal dispute sitting down with a neutral third party to help resolve the problem by compromise. In a divorce case, a mediator would work with you and your husband to try to settle matters of child custody and visitation, property division and support.

Some people turn to mediation because they think it's the only alternative to a knock-down-drag-out court fight. In fact, as we've seen, most family law disputes never go to court but are settled instead by lawyer-negotiated agreements. The few cases that actually do go to court are generally those in which one or both of the parties absolutely refuse to compromise. So while neither lawyers nor mediators are *always* successful in persuading the parties to compromise and avoid a court fight, both are in fact able to do so in most cases.

In other words, the basic choice you are making is not

between mediation and fighting it out in court. Your choice is whether to seek a negotiated settlement (with lawyers doing the negotiation) or a mediated settlement (with you and your husband negotiating in the presence of a mediator).

HOW MEDIATION AND
NEGOTIATION DIFFER

One important difference between a traditional lawyer and a mediator is that the lawyer is paid to be your advocate, while a mediator is paid to be impartial. Thus, in a traditional negotiation situation, your lawyer would try to guard your rights and get the best possible deal for you, while the noncustodial parent's lawyer did the same for him.

In mediation, the mediator's official function is simply to help the parties to reach an agreement that both will accept and follow. While most mediators try to forge an agreement that will be fair to both parents, that's not really their job. Mediators, unlike traditional lawyers, have no duty to advise either parent on how best to protect their rights and interests in a case.

Many people who favor mediation feel it appeals to the parties' better natures, encouraging them to resolve their differences in a cooperative rather than a competitive manner. In many cases, that's true—as long as there's honest good faith on both sides. In families where both parents place a high priority on the welfare of the children, mediation can be a good setting for working out the details of how they'll be raised. Parents can discuss openly their ideas about such matters as visitation, the children's education, and so on, helping both to feel involved in the child-raising process.

In some cases, that sense of mutual involvement will induce one parent to be more generous to and understanding of the other than might otherwise have been possible. Because the two parents help shape the agreement themselves, they may also respect and follow it more reliably.

Some families find that mediation can help them to explore and resolve their feelings about a new family situation as they work actively to restructure it. Divorce or separation is a major life change, and when mediation works well it can provide a reassuring sense of control over one's life. In that respect, it's a little bit like going for family separation therapy.

It should be understood, however, that these happy results are likely *only* in cases where both parents are truly concerned, involved, and ready to place the children's needs above their own. Unfortunately, that's often not the case. All too often—as anger, defensiveness, or even simple selfishness come into play—mediation can be used to gain an unfair bargaining advantage.

Some women who favor openness and cooperation nonetheless find mediation too risky. They might suggest family separation counseling to help create an atmosphere of greater trust and respect. They might urge their lawyers to avoid hostile tactics. Yet for actual negotiations, they feel safer with the more traditional legal setting.

WHY MEDIATION CAN BE DANGEROUS

The mediator is not your advocate, and has no obligation to advise you of your legal rights or of the consequences of a settlement agreement. That means that you could bargain away valuable rights without ever realizing you were doing so.

For example, many mediators openly favor joint custody, and in fact, most mediated agreements do feature joint custody arrangements. While joint custody may be right for some families, it is certainly a decision with serious legal and practical consequences. It would be the legal duty of any attorney representing you in a divorce case to explain how agreeing to joint custody could create problems in terms of decreased child support, less control over decisions regarding your child, or a custody conflict should you later need to move to a new state. A mediator would have no duty to explain these things, and might feel that discussing them would interfere with the goal of reaching a compromise.

Actually, some mediators don't even know much about the legal consequences of divorce agreements. Many are mental health professionals with little or no training in law. Others, on the other hand, are lawyers with little or no training in counseling. And because there are now no licensing requirements for mediators in most states, some have little professional training in either field.

Of course, you can minimize the risk of unwittingly trading away important rights by consulting carefully with your lawyer before you begin mediation, and checking in again after each session. Yet suppose, talking with your lawyer after a mediation session, you learn you've just agreed to give up rights you didn't realize were important. You're probably not legally bound as long as you haven't signed anything, but it could be difficult to backtrack in the bargaining.

There's also an important practical problem with mediation, in that a mediator must, to gain the trust of both sides, avoid any appearance of partiality. This is fine if both parties are equally reasonable in their suggestions and requests, but it can create problems if there's an imbalance or a lack of good faith.

For example, suppose you were to start out making a fair and reasonable proposal, while the children's father made an unreasonable one. Had you privately told an attorney your goals, she or he might have said, "Well, that sounds fair. I'll ask for a little bit more and let them bargain me down." Had your husband done the same, his attorney might well have replied, "I'm sorry, but there's no way I can get you anywhere near that." Each lawyer would then have entered the bargaining arena with a proposal weighted slightly toward his or her client, but ready to compromise to reach a reasonable agreement.

If instead you enter mediation with a fair proposal, while the children's father makes a totally unfair one, the mediator will have a hard time getting much cooperation by saying, "Well, Mr. Jones, now that I've heard both sides, I really think you ought to agree to everything Ms. Jones suggests." More likely, another kind of "compromise" will result—one somewhere in between your fair proposal and the father's unfair one.

As you can see, there's a very basic problem here. You are urged, in mediation, to be fair, cooperative, even generous in resolving disputes. Yet, as this example shows, if one person tries to be fair and the other doesn't, mediation may actually reward the unfair one.

MALE/FEMALE POWER IMBALANCES

Any form of bargaining, to work well, requires roughly equal power between the two sides. That's why, for example, an individual laborer would not sit down to bargain over wage contracts with a large industrial employer. Instead, the employees band together in a union, hoping to equalize the power balance and get a fairer deal.

In domestic law mediation, there is an assumption of equal bargaining power that is often unrealistic. As Joanne Schulman, formerly of the National Center on Women and Family Law, explains it, "There are any number of factors which can create inequality between the parties. Overwhelmingly, they're factors which tend to favor men over women."

Men frequently have greater income and career mobility, more extensive knowledge of family financial holdings, and they may view any earnings or assets as "their" money. They may be more experienced at bargaining and more willing to use power and control tactics. Women, however, are more likely to be the primary caretaker of the child or children, and may place a high priority upon not angering the father. They may also have less experience or encouragement in expressing their own needs and ideas, or may hope to restore peace in the family by not making too many demands.

Particularly if you've been the children's primary caretaker and have limited financial resources, mediation could place you in a constant defensive position. In fact, you'll be supporting the children within your household and are asking only that the father contribute his fair share. If you are seeking alimony, it's in exchange for the work you've done and will continue to do raising your mutual children. Yet because you're asking for a sum of money—and because the work of child raising is so often undervalued in our society—you may be unfairly characterized as asking for some sort of gift or charity. It could be harder for you to argue your cause in mediation than it would be for your lawyer to argue it in negotiation.

Before you agree to mediation, you should think carefully about whether any of the following questions apply to you:

- Are you the children's primary caretaker, and will you continue to be?
- Do you earn less or have more limited career opportunities than the children's father?
- Is the children's father more informed about financial or legal matters than you are, or more experienced at bargaining?
- Do you ever (or often) find yourself giving in to demands you know are unfair simply because it's too difficult or too unpleasant to persist?
- Do you ever feel afraid of or intimidated by the children's father?
- Do you find that conversations tend to be dominated by him, in that he seems to talk more and listen less?

Each one of these questions signals a possible problem area in terms of bargaining power. For every "yes" answer, you'll want to think carefully about whether mediation is right for you.

Yet while some mediators don't recognize a power imbalance problem, others believe that trying to equalize the scales is part of a mediator's job. "I work to empower the weaker party in mediation," explains Boston area mediator Diane Neumann. "An agreement isn't any good unless it's fair."

Neumann believes that the power imbalance problem can actually be worse with lawyers doing the negotiating than with a good mediator. "People tend to choose lawyers based on their own personality types. If an angry, controlling man goes out and hires a high-powered, no-holds-barred lawyer, while his timid wife goes out and hires a timid lawyer, that makes things worse. Buf if I as a mediator can say, 'Wait a minute, you've said your piece, now listen to your wife's side,' that can help."

It's a judgment call much like the question of how aggressive a lawyer to choose. In the best case, mediation can help guide both parties toward a reasonable settlement, with a skilled mediator intervening to stop attempted power plays. In the worst case, it can give an angry husband more opportunity to directly intimidate his wife into accepting an unfair settlement. Only you can decide, based on your own gut-level feeling about how you and your husband interact, whether mediation is a possibility for you. Then, if it is, you'll have to choose a mediator carefully.

There are some circumstances in which you should *never* agree to mediation. If the children's father has been violent toward you or the children or been sexually abusive toward a child, mediation is not a good choice. Simply stated, you can't bargain freely with someone who threatens you. You need the full protection of the law to keep yourself and your children safe, and a good lawyer to put some distance between you and the children's father during negotiations. Abusers are not motivated by what's fair, and they are famous for manipulating unwary professionals (not to mention their wives) with expressions of remorse and promises to do better.

You should also avoid mediation if you suspect that your husband may have income, benefits, or other assets that he's trying to hide and avoid sharing. As you'll learn in Chapter 5, there are many ways to combat this common problem and discover the hidden assets. Very few of these methods, however, are effective in the mediation setting.

Clearly, your role in mediation is a delicate one. You're expected to be cooperative and generous, but must also protect your rights and provide for your children's needs. You need to trust the other parent enough to be flexible, but must not trust blindly or when the trust hasn't been earned. It's a tricky balance in the best of cases, and only you can decide if it's right for you.

IF YOU DECIDE TO MEDIATE

If you favor mediation's cooperative approach to problem solving and have a basic sense of trust in the fairness and honesty of the children's father, you may wish to try it. If so, you'll want to follow some simple steps to use it as safely and wisely as possible.

The first and really unavoidable step will still be to start with your lawyer. Ask about your rights in the case, what would be a likely result from the traditional legal route, and what you should consider as you bargain. If there are potential problems that make your case ill suited to mediation, your lawyer should alert you to them. Also, since you'll have to file court papers and have a judge approve any agreement you make, your lawyer can help you with that.

Above all, you should have any agreement checked over by your lawyer (*not* just a lawyer acting as or with the mediator) before you sign or agree to anything. This is important to be sure both that the agreement doesn't violate your rights and that it meets legal requirements of clarity and form. Most mediators are not lawyers, and even small mistakes can create problems later.

You should be aware that some lawyers discourage clients from working with mediators, or overcharge for their own part of the job when a mediator is used. That's why, if you know you hope to mediate, you should choose a lawyer who is used to cooperating with mediators.

If, after discussing your case with your lawyer, you feel mediation is right for you, your next step will be choosing a mediator. (Since the choice of a mediator is the first thing you and your husband will need to agree on, that means working together on the project.) Possibly your lawyer will know of some reputable mediators, or a friend you trust may be able to recommend one. Mediation services are frequently listed in the telephone yellow pages under "Mediation," "Divorce," or "Counseling," but a personal recommendation is always preferable.

The first questions you'll need to ask, before even scheduling a first appointment, are about background and training. This is essential, for a very important reason. Because domestic law mediation is a fairly new field, most states have no legal requirements for mediators or procedures for licensing. This means it's up to you to be certain you are comfortable with the mediator's credentials. If you have any doubts or hesitations, you'd be wise to trust them and keep looking.

Many mediators are trained and licensed as psychologists, clinical social workers, or lawyers. Since all of these professions have licensing and disciplinary boards, you should check with the appropriate state board to be sure that the mediator you're considering is a member in good standing and has no outstanding disciplinary complaints on file. If your state has a separate licensing board for mediators (few do), check with that board too.

Another essential matter you'll want to ask about in advance is cost. While you probably won't be quoted a package price (since the total hours of mediation needed will depend in part on how quickly agreement is reached), the mediator should be able to quote you hourly rates. Most mediators can also give you ballpark figures of how long average cases of your type usually take to resolve. While these figures will give you only an estimate or a cost range, they are helpful in comparing costs with other mediators.

When estimating mediation costs, remember to include your lawyer's fees and court costs. You may find that mediation is still less expensive than the traditional route. That's because negotiation, the most time-consuming part of domestic law, tends to go faster in mediation. Also, in lawyer-assisted negotiation, two lawyers are being paid for every hour they negotiate together; while in mediation sessions, only one mediator is being paid. (The cost of the mediator is usually split between the parties or taken from the marital property.)

Questions about training and cost can be handled over the phone with the mediator's office. Then, when you go for a first appointment, you'll be able to focus more on questions about the mediator's attitudes and methods.

One subject you'll want to find out about is the mediator's attitudes toward families. Some mediators (male or female) accept social stereotypes that the family money is the man's money, and support to the children chivalrous but not a matter of right. Others—perhaps more—may be so forward-thinking that they assume a level of cooperation and shared work that doesn't yet exist in most cases. They may, for example, assume that the children's father will share equally in child raising, and that you will have ample career opportunities. If this isn't your family situation, that assumption can hurt you.

You might also want to ask whether the mediator thinks there can be power imbalances in a family, and how they can affect mediation. The answer may be very interesting and will tell you a lot about what to expect. Be wary of any mediator who seems irritated by your question, or insists that the problem doesn't exist.

If your husband is present during this first meeting, you'll want to be especially careful about how you ask these questions. "What kind of families do you usually see?" is less controversial than "Do you think men today are really involved in child care the way mothers are?" Yet with a little fishing, you'll get a sense of the mediator's attitudes.

Once you have chosen a mediator and are about to begin the process, take some time to consider your mediation goals. Write down what you hope to accomplish and discuss your ideas with your lawyer. Think about which issues are negotiable and which you see as non-negotiable. The more clear you are in your own mind about what you and your children need, the more likely you are to meet those goals.

During the course of the mediation, try to be as businesslike as possible. Avoid unnecessary arguments, but don't hesitate to express concerns about the fairness or practicality of any proposal. Be honest about your feelings, but try to avoid letting emotional responses dominate the sessions. Instead, focus on your mediation goals, stating your opinions as calmly and confidently as you can.

Because bargaining is bargaining, you should start by asking for what you think would be a *very* agreeable arrangement—and then be ready to negotiate downward if need be. Possibly your lawyer can help you to strategize.

You should be aware that the mediation process does not yet have many of the legal protections that have developed over the years to protect people during lawyer-assisted negotiation. For example, if you were to reveal private information during a lawyer-assisted negotiation session, it could not later be used against you in court. Yet it could be used against you if your slip was during a mediation session. That may not be a reason in itself to avoid mediation, but it probably means you should avoid discussing such things as a new sexual relationship in your life or serious emotional difficulties you're having.

Additionally, the current lack of professional standards and disciplinary boards specifically for mediators can affect not only your choice of a mediator but also the handling of your case. You'll have less leverage for protesting actions or policies that you feel are unprofessional or unfair, while the mediator has less peer guidance for conducting cases. Though this will probably change with time, as the profession develops, for now it is your responsibility to be sure you are satisfied with the fairness of mediation at every point.

Finally, keep in mind that you can withdraw from private mediation at any time you decide you're unhappy with either the mediator or the process. Just as your lawyer keeps a stronger stance in negotiation by quietly communicating that she or he is ready to go to court if need be, you will be stronger in mediation if it's clear that you want to compromise but will leave if your rights or the children's welfare is being compromised.

Note, however, that you may not have quite the same freedom to withdraw in a mediation office associated with the court. That is, you might withdraw, but not without an unfavorable report and recommendation sent directly from the mediator to the judge. This can be very dangerous to your case and is a good reason to be especially cautious before agreeing to participate in court-affiliated mediation.

POWER AND EMPOWERMENT

In custody and related financial negotiations, you have to plan ahead. You're restructuring your family life with someone who may or may not share your vision and ideas.

Whether you stick with lawyer-assisted negotiation or try mediation, this is an important opportunity to learn and grow. It's an opportunity to be empowered in reshaping your own life.

Read all you can. Ask plenty of questions. Share your ideas freely. Above all, remember that any professionals you hire work for you—*not* the other way around.

4 ☐ DEVELOPING A CUSTODY PLAN

Many people think that the first thing they need to decide about custody is who will get it. It's not. In fact, when you work on developing and negotiating a custody plan, your first priority should be the practical question of how to divide the day-to-day care of the children. The legal question of who will then have legal custody rights is the *last* issue you should decide or even discuss.

If that seems surprising, think about it from your child's point of view. Your child's concerns are very basic: Where will I sleep? Who will cook my breakfast? Who will buy my clothes? How will I spend my weekends? Will Mom and Dad still love me?

All of these are very practical, very specific, and, from your child's perspective, absolutely crucial questions. They need and deserve to be answered. While they are certainly related to the question of who will have custody, note that they are not answered by it. Telling your children, "I'll be your legal custodian," does not say where they'll be sleeping on Saturday night.

There's another very important reason to look at the day-to-day practical questions first. For the most part, they are less emotionally loaded than the final custody decision. Yet if you take care of the little decisions, sometimes the bigger decisions become much easier.

Jim Tanner and Gail Bartley are parents who learned this the hard way. When Gail and Jim were getting a divorce, each hired a lawyer, but they decided to do most of their negotiating on their own. Because the welfare of their ten-year-old daughter, Sarah, was a high priority to both of them, they started with a discussion of who should have custody.

Almost immediately, they found themselves at an impasse. Carefully, trying not to offend, Gail explained that she felt it was best if she had custody. She had really been caring for Sarah since birth, and now they were especially close, enjoying quiet talks and special projects together when Jim was out of town. Ever since Jim's promotion to senior account executive two years ago, Gail reminded him, he'd been less and less active a parent.

Jim was stung. He loved Sarah every bit as much as Gail did, and Gail knew it. He hated having to travel and had even complained about it to his boss. But Gail was trying to make him out to be a nonparent, a nobody. If he agreed now to give Gail custody, it would be like saying he didn't care about Sarah.

Jim became insistent: If Gail didn't immediately consent to joint custody, he would seek full custody. Rather than risk a custody fight, Gail reluctantly agreed. Against her better judgment, she also agreed that there would be no child support, since they'd be sharing Sarah's care. The whole thing worried her, because as a teacher she had more free time to care for Sarah but earned much less than Jim.

Ultimately, the arrangement created a strain on them all. Jim, although anxious to prove himself just as involved a parent as Gail, still had to travel during the week. Thinking he'd make the most of the weekends, he said he'd care for Sarah each week from Friday evening to Sunday evening.

He quickly discovered that meant no weekend time to himself, no time to rest from a hard week of traveling, and little or no opportunity to date. He'd also never realized how much energy and attention one child can demand in a twenty-four-hour day. Against his will, he began to feel resentful and trapped.

Gail, meanwhile, was missing Sarah terribly on the weekends. She resented the fact that she'd done all the work getting Sarah out of diapers, and was still doing the work getting her off to school all week, but Jim (as she saw it) was having all the fun weekend times with Sarah.

Nor was Sarah very happy with the arrangement. She

liked all the sudden attention from her father, but she missed her mother on weekends. Plus there was something that bothered her a lot. Dad and Mom both said they wanted her with them, but they seemed mad all the time she was around. That scared her.

A big part of the problem was that Gail and Jim had started their custody discussion at the end instead of the beginning. By asking first, "Who should get custody?" they immediately got locked into a struggle of egos. As soon as Gail said she thought she should have custody, Jim heard it as a criticism of him. He was so anxious to disprove the criticism that he insisted on a role that wasn't realistic. Gail, for her part, had so alienated him with her first statement that she was afraid to bring up any new concerns.

Eventually, some three years and much frustration later, Jim and Gail were able to admit that the plan wasn't working and start over. Jim loved Sarah, but their weekends had become too pressured to enjoy. He proposed that Sarah spend from Saturday morning to midday Sunday with him, and that they talk on the phone regularly during the week. Recognizing that Gail's expenses were greater, and that her taking responsibility for Sarah was once again allowing him more time to pursue his career, he finally agreed to pay child support. After much soul searching, he even agreed that, with Gail actually caring for Sarah six days a week, it did make sense to name her as the legal custodian.

Note that when we talk about child custody arrangements, we're actually talking about two very separate things: child-raising responsibility and the legal assignment of custody rights. Child-raising responsibility is what your children will think and ask about: Who will take care of them when? The legal assignment of custody has more to do with parents' legal rights. Legal custody says who has the legal right to make decisions about the children, including decisions about where they will live, where they'll go to school, and what rules they'll follow. Ideally, legal custody rights are assigned in a way that will support the parent or parents with actual responsibility in caring for, guiding, and protecting the children.

It's generally best to follow this step-by-step approach to making custody decisions:

Step One: First, look at the pattern of family responsibility—what each of you has actually contributed to child raising and family life—in the past.

Step Two: Next, decide what future child-raising arrangements are practical and likely to be in the children's best interests, drawing heavily from your knowledge of what's worked in the past.

Step Three: Your last decision should be about legal custody, because the question of parental rights can better be decided when it's clear who will have what parental responsibilities.

You'll note that this decision-making process stresses above all *continuity of care* for the children. You start by looking at what's been the child-raising pattern in the past, then you use it as a guide when developing a custody plan for the future.

This is because your children need as much stability as possible during and after a family separation. Even under the best of circumstances, they will already have to adjust to a number of major changes. To add to that upheaval by creating a sudden switch in child-raising arrangements is to invite a greater sense of loss and insecurity. Even if both parents are *potentially* equally skilled at child raising, a sudden change, for example, from Mom's care to Dad's care (or to Dad's new wife's care) will feel like a tremendous loss of security to a child.

A child's need for continuity of care has been well documented by social science research. In a major three-volume study of a child's attachment to a caregiver, *Attachment and Loss,*[30] psychiatrist John Bowlby found that a child, from infancy on, forms a principal attachment to that person who is most responsive to the child's biological and social needs. If the child is abruptly separated from the caregiver, severe anxiety and lasting emotional difficulties develop.

In 1973, Joseph Goldstein, Anna Freud, and Albert Solnit published the influential work, *Beyond the Best Interests of the Child*.[31] Applying social science concepts to the custody decision process, the authors emphasized the overwhelming importance of continuity of care in a child's life, explaining that adults often fail to understand and respect this need in children. Yet, once a child forms an emotional attachment to a primary caretaker—described by the authors as the "psychological parent"—it is crucial to the child's continued mental health to preserve that bond.

Goldstein, Freud, and Solnit deplored insensitive custody policies which failed to safeguard that primary psychological bond. They described the harmful effects upon children of various ages who were abruptly separated from their "psychological parent": infants tended to suffer separation distress, and to become less trustful in their next attachments; young children suffered setbacks in their ability to achieve and be social; and even adolescents, who seem eager for independence, suffered anxiety and damaged self-esteem.

Both of these works emphasized as most important the bond between the child and a primary caregiver, who was usually the natural or adoptive mother. More recent works have recognized that in families where child care is divided between more than one adult, the child may have more than one important attachment.[32] On one point, however, the experts agree: Whatever the patterns and attachments of caregiving before the family separation, it is best to avoid sudden, extreme disruption to them.[33]

Some changes, of course, may be necessary or desirable. You may also find that you have to be a bit flexible to negotiate well. For those reasons, as we look at each step toward developing a custody plan, we'll use the continuity-of-care standard only as a guide.

The decision-making process described here can be used whether you and the children's father are negotiating with the help of your attorneys or before a mediator. You can suggest it even if the lawyer or mediator does not. For example, if your lawyer says, "We'll start by deciding who will have custody of the children," you could say, "Well, that sounds good, but I want to avoid presenting it as a competition. I think it would help if we first look at what we've done in the past, and then use that as a guide for the future."

STEP ONE: LOOKING AT PAST CONTRIBUTIONS TO FAMILY LIFE

Quite likely, in your family, you and the children's father have each contributed differently to the family welfare. When you begin to look at past family patterns, it's important to keep in mind that different doesn't necessarily mean better or worse. Right now, in the midst of hurt and anger over the separation, it may not be easy to give credit to your soon-to-be-ex for the positive ways he's influenced the children's lives. (This is particularly so if he's not giving you credit for your important role in the family.) Yet even if his contribution has been *only* financial—and probably it's been more—that's valuable in itself.

There are important reasons beyond simple fairness for this emphasis. First, your children will benefit if their father stays emotionally and financially involved with them. Acknowledging past contributions is one way to help encourage future ones.

It can also help prevent a custody fight. Consider the example of Jim and Gail above. During the marriage, Jim *was* contributing: a (very) little bit of regular child care, some special weekend times with Sarah, and a lot of financial support. Yet when the conversation seemed focused almost entirely on child care, where Jim was weakest, he became defensive. He felt he had to prove himself as a parent—if necessary, by fighting for custody.

It can help, then, before even talking about the future, for each parent to take a few minutes to acknowledge the other's contributions to family life. "I've noticed that you often take the kids to the playground on Saturdays," you might say. "They really seem to enjoy it." Or, "I know I've sometimes complained about your long work hours, but I must say you've really worked hard and been a good provider."

This should be an exchange, with each of you taking turns. Try to be positive and honest, but don't go on and on with praise that's undeserved or not returned. (Excessive praise could come back to haunt you: "Why, Judge, even she says I'm better with the kids than she is.") The idea is simply to credit one another's contributions to family life, with an eye to planning for them to continue. As each comment is offered, it should be written down for future reference.

Don't worry if you feel you've made important contributions that the children's father doesn't mention. At this point, you're simply emphasizing areas of appreciation and agreement, not trying to make a complete list of who does what.

The next step should be to try to get a sense of the everyday fabric of life: How do you each generally spend your time? You can start informally, with each of you discussing your usual schedule in general terms.

It's a good idea to let the children's father go first. He may say something like: "Well, on a weekday I might have time for breakfast, but usually it's straight to work. I start at nine, work until six-thirty or seven, then come home for dinner. After dinner, I help the kids with their homework or maybe read them a story. Then they go to bed and I read or watch TV or go for a walk before quitting for the night."

Such an account is honest, and it certainly describes a hard worker. Knowing that his contributions are recognized, this man can feel comfortable. Yet he hasn't thought a lot about how breakfast and dinner were cooked, who helped the children get ready for school or for bed, who was responsible for them before 7:00 P.M., and so on. As the mother briefly describes her schedule, that will become clear. Later, if he's so inclined, it will be harder for him to say, "Oh, we split child care chores equally."

Once you've each described your weekdays and weekends, you should have a fairly complete picture of your family life. If possible, get an agreement that your account is accurate. You should also say whether you agree with the father's account and why. Avoid judgmental statements like: "That's not true! You never cook dinner." A more effective comment might be: "I don't agree that we share cooking. While it's true that you often make the salad, I'm almost always responsible for planning and cooking dinners during the week."

In most cases, despite a little exaggeration on both sides, a relatively clear picture of daily life emerges. Possibly, the accounts will point out some contributions by one or both parents that weren't mentioned in the list compiled at the beginning of the conversation. If so, they should be added to the list.

Ideally, your lawyer should help identify contributions of yours that should be noted, or a mediator should point out major contributions of both parents. If that doesn't happen, it's up to you. It's perfectly appropriate at this point to say something like: "Let's look at the list of parent contributions again. Since we've now agreed that I'm the one who usually feeds, bathes, and changes the baby, I'd like to see that added to the list."

If caretaking patterns in your family have recently changed, you'll want to present a fuller picture that includes past contributions. Perhaps when the children were young you cared for them full time, and sought a paid job only after the youngest was in day care or school. Or perhaps the separation itself has created new responsibilities as you look for a better-paying job or a new apartment, so that recently you've been less available to the children. Yet the years that you cared for your children on an intensive daily basis aren't over and forgotten in your child's mind. An important, central relationship was built then and remains important now. Emphasize that as you discuss family child-raising patterns, to make sure your role with the children over the years is recognized.

This step of the negotiation process need not take a long time or result in an exhaustive list of family responsibilities. The idea is simply to get a basic, shared recognition of past family child-raising patterns.

STEP TWO: DEVELOPING AND
NEGOTIATING A CHILD-RAISING PLAN

Once you have examined past family patterns, your next step will be to develop a child-raising plan for the future. It should be as specific as possible, so that it's clear who will have what responsibilities. When your child asks: "Who will help me shop for clothes?" "Where will I spend Saturday nights?" or "Who will take me to soccer practice?" you'll have the answers.

Your child's need for stability and continuity should affect your planning in two ways. First, your child-raising plan should disturb the present parent-child relationships as little as possible. Second, it should offer the children a reasonably stable lifestyle in the future.

This can require creative thinking, with everyone's schedule taken into account. You want to keep the parent-child relationships stable, yet the split into two households means that some changes are necessary. Think about ways to preserve the *spirit* of the relationships, even if some daily habits must change.

The child-raising plan is the most personal part of all the negotiating you will do throughout the separation process. While you'll want to remember basic bargaining techniques discussed in Chapter 3 (such as not starting with the least favorable offer you're willing to accept), you shouldn't be bound by them. The best way to develop a child-raising plan is through honest cooperation between parents, if at all possible. Sometimes a parent who will fight about every other aspect of a divorce—property rights and even legal custody rights—can be persuaded to cooperate in planning for day-to-day care of the children.

A common mistake in setting up a child-raising plan is to attempt to divide time between parents exactly equally, without considering the effect on the children and their schedules. For example, parents will agree to take the children every other week, month, or even year, not realizing how jolting it is for a child to be regularly uprooted. Or they will agree to each take the children three and a half days a week, not considering that this divides the children's school week in half. These are agreements that emphasize parents' rights, not children's needs.

Commonly, these arrangements also don't reflect the family patterns established during the marriage. If your list from Step One shows that you've been the major child raiser while the father has provided a great deal of the financial support, a sharp fifty-fifty child-raising plan after divorce would disrupt that lifestyle.

Even if shared child-raising responsibility is appropriate for your family, it's best to fashion a plan that considers the children's need for a stable home base. One divorcing couple, Marian and Tom, developed a sensitive plan for doing this.

Marian, a nurse-midwife, and Tom, a Head Start director, had always shared child-raising responsibility for their three (now school-age) children. When they divorced, they agreed that they would continue to share responsibility, but that the children should have one place where they usually went home to sleep. Because Marian's work meant that she was on call two nights a week, they agreed that that home should be Tom's.

Under the plan, the children spent six nights a week in their home with Tom and a Saturday overnight with Marian. Additionally, Marian arranged to leave work early and have the children over for a leisurely dinner each Monday, Tuesday, and Thursday.

"The hardest thing about this plan," says Marian, "was agreeing to it. At first I thought, 'They'll be Tom's kids, living with him.' Plus it meant giving up living in the house and getting an apartment nearby, since Tom would need to keep up the kids' bedrooms.

"As it's turned out, though, they spend three weekday evenings and all day and night Saturday with me, and two weekday evenings and all day and night Sunday with Tom. The rest of the time they're sleeping or rushing off to school, so why should I make an issue of where they sleep? They feel more secure this way. It's also more practical in terms of space: With them sleeping over just once a week, they can share one room and think it's a slumber party."

Marian is aware that there's a risk in this plan. If she or Tom later decides to move out of state, she faces a serious chance of losing her active role with the children. She could seek sole custody at that time, but it would be an uphill battle. Quite possibly, a judge would view her as a less involved, possibly even negligent mother. (In a classic double standard, judges often view half-time fathers as wonderfully involved, but half-time mothers as shamefully uninvolved.) Yet because Marian trusts Tom, because both parents are committed to staying in the area, and because the plan seems best for the children now, Marian is willing to take the risk.

If you have been your children's primary caretaker, you can best protect their stability by negotiating an arrangement with your home as the primary base. Yet, as Marian's experience shows, both parents can stay highly involved whatever the home base.

Equal or near equal child-raising responsibility is a wonderful goal, but not right for every separated family. It requires good communication and cooperation between parents, strong parent-child relationships, and children flexible enough to adjust to a role in two households. Younger children may resist because they need more stability in their life, while older children and teenagers may have activities of their own that conflict with time scheduled with each parent.

It can also create economic hardship. Few families can afford to set up two households with rooms for the children, toys, books, and so on. What often happens is that the decision to share child-raising leads to the sale of the family home (with proceeds split equally) and little or no child support. Often, then, the father—but not the mother—can afford to recreate a suitable family home. In the worst cases, the father enjoys the financial benefits but slowly tapers off his involvement in child raising. The children end up actually living in a cramped apartment with the mother, and visiting their father in a more comfortable, roomy home.

In general, the risks involved in shared parenting after divorce are greatest when there is no history of shared responsibility during the marriage. It's best, therefore, to move slowly in making changes, again avoiding sudden disruptions in family patterns. (You especially don't want to risk *two* abrupt changes—one when the father takes on a major new role, and a second when he decides the new role isn't working and cuts back his involvement.) Instead, try to develop a plan that will gradually increase the father's role in child raising. Such an arrangement can enrich the children's lives as they grow closer to their father, and enrich your life as you enjoy some occasional free time.

Don Roberts, for example, is a concerned father who benefitted from a plan involving slow increases in his time with his children. Don was an only child, whose own father had been dignified and distant. Don dearly loved his two sons, aged two and five, and enjoyed playing with them and reading to them. Yet he'd never dressed, bathed, or fed them, in part out of nervousness that he'd do it wrong.

After the divorce, Don enrolled in a parenting class and began talking with other fathers and mothers, learning that most were also nervous at first. Over a period of six months, he built up from three-hour Saturday visits to all weekend every other weekend. During his summer vacation, he had the children with him for most of the two weeks.

For a father who was almost totally uninvolved in child raising during the marriage, of course, shared parenting after the divorce simply isn't realistic. Regular child-father contact should still be encouraged, however, and structured into the plan.

"Even children whose fathers were distant and preoccupied during the marriage talk about missing their fathers terribly after divorce," explains Judith Wallerstein, child psychoanalyst and coauthor of the influential *Surviving the Breakup: How Children and Parents Cope with Divorce* (Basic Books, 1980). "They worry about why the father is gone, and their self-esteem suffers. If the fathers can be helped and supported in strengthening the relationship instead of disappearing, the child benefits."

It's good advice, although it can be hard to follow. Many mothers feel they've done everything possible to encourage an active role by a father who simply won't respond. Others find it hard to encourage a relationship when they are so personally angry with the father. Still others wonder if the father's shortcomings, such as undependability or lack of obvious warmth, won't make him a negative influence.

Do the best you can. You can encourage involvement, but you can't force it. As for any anger or concern about faults you may have, these are natural. Yet it's important to be as honest and objective as you can. You may be angry, but your child identifies closely with both parents. All parents have faults, and children learn to live with those faults. When contact ends between parent and child, the child is likely to feel rejected and guilty, even if *you* know the child is not at fault. Unless the father is abusive or neglectful, even a very imperfect father is generally better for your child than no father at all.

Sometimes, in structuring a child-raising plan, there's an impulse to be competitive, to worry that if the children grow closer to their father, they'll take sides against you. If that happens to you, try to talk about those feelings with a friend or counselor away from the negotiating, so that they won't enter into the negotiations.

Your children really do have room in their hearts for two parents. In fact, if they can maintain both relationships, they'll probably be more trusting and affectionate in all their relationships. It's an interesting fact about parenting that sometimes, in letting go, you actually become closer.

Finally, in structuring your plan, make sure that you allow some flexibility for the future. As your children grow, their needs may change. Your ten-year-old may be happy to spend his Saturday evenings with a parent now, but in a few years he'll be more interested in Saturday night school dances. At that point, schedules may have to be adjusted so that no relationship suffers.

In sum, your goal in this step is simply to plan a practical way to care for the children, with each parent taking responsibilities similar to past ones. If an increased role by the father is a family goal, the change should be gradual rather than abrupt.

STEP THREE: ASSIGNING LEGAL CUSTODY RIGHTS

After you've agreed upon a child-raising plan, you'll need to agree about custody rights. Although these are parental rights, your focus should still be on the best interests of the children. Basically, custody rights are a necessary and important tool to guarantee that a parent with *responsibility for child raising* will also have the *right to make decisions about child raising*.

You have three options for legal custody: custody in the mother, custody in the father, or joint custody.

If the mother or the father is named as the custodian, that parent will have the right to make general decisions about where the child will live and go to school, what type of medical care the child will get, what rules the child will follow, and so on. That doesn't mean, however, that the other parent will have no rights. The noncustodial parent will be entitled to see the child at the times specified in your child-raising plan (generally called "visitation rights"), will be able to authorize emergency medical care for the child as needed, and will as a practical matter determine rules for the child during visitation times.

If you agree to joint custody, both parents will have an equal voice in all decisions about the children. If a major decision arises and you can't agree, you'll have to ask the judge to decide for you. This can be expensive and disruptive, and means that joint custody is a realistic possibility only when the parents have a very good ability to make decisions and work out differences together.

As a general rule, it's best if legal custody reflects the actual physical custody arrangements practiced under the child-raising plan. That is, custody in one parent is appropriate if that parent will have the major responsibility for child raising. Joint custody is only appropriate if the parents are truly sharing child-raising responsibility (and if they communicate and make decisions well together). Thus, Step Three simply involves looking at what you've already developed under Step Two and giving the most accurate name to it.

Sometimes mothers think that it's kinder to call the arrangement joint custody even if they will be taking primary responsibility for the children. Maybe so, but that sentiment can be expensive and perhaps dangerous to your family's stability. There are several reasons why it is important to insist on an accurate assignment of legal custody rights.

First, if you will be primarily caring for the children, legal custody will protect your right to make decisions about their care without fear of interference. If, for example, your child asks for permission to engage in a sport you consider dangerous, you'll be the one nursing that child back to health if she or he is injured. You also are the only one with the daily opportunity to observe your child's physical abilities and vulnerabilities. Possibly, you have some insight into whether the child is responding to peer pressure or really feels interested and confident. Under these circumstances, you can best protect your child if you have the authority to make the decision.

Another decision you might need to make on your own is where you and the children will live. Although some states require a parent with custody to get permission from the other parent or the judge in order to move to another state, this is uncommon. If you have joint custody, however, it is much more likely that you'll need this permission. (Laws vary by state, so check with your lawyer.)

Finances are another reason to seek an accurate assignment of custody. As a general rule, it's hard to negotiate adequate property division and support if legal custody is described as joint. Even if you'll actually be doing most of the child raising, the attitude tends to be: "Well, it's joint custody, so why should she get the house? Why should he pay child support?"

Finally, legal custody that accurately reflects actual child raising is important in protecting against later disruptions to family life. For example, a common trend is for fathers to be relatively uninvolved in child care directly after a divorce, but to seek custody if they remarry. A judge at that time might feel that the remarried father can offer the children greater stability than the single mother, but would probably also have some concern about disruption to the children.

If, however, the postdivorce arrangement had been called joint custody, the judge might assume that the father had actually been involved in child raising all along. "Well," the judge might think, "with joint custody this child has been shuttled back and forth, but now if I give the father custody, things will be more stable." Thus, a destabilizing move from one household to another would appear to a judge to be stabilizing, simply because the original arrangement was misnamed.

Because an accurate assignment of custody rights is so crucial, it's important that legal custody also not be assigned on the basis of promises. Suppose, for example, that the father has not been heavily involved in child raising in the past but promises to increase his role in the future. (You'll recall from the last section that this change should be gradual.) In that case, joint legal custody would be appropriate only when the plan became a working reality. The way to do this is to assign temporary legal custody in the mother, with an agreement to change it to permanent joint custody *if and only if* child-raising responsibility begins to be truly shared.

You should be aware, however, that this is an advocacy position. Not uncommonly, fathers who will not be heavily involved in child raising nonetheless want the rights associated with custody or joint custody. They are helped, in many states, by laws that encourage joint custody awards whether or not child-raising responsibility is actually shared.

You and your lawyer may have to advocate vigorously on the basis of fairness and stability for the children. The concept in this step is quite simple, but you may have to repeat it often: Just assign custody rights to match the child-raising responsibility.

Negotiating a positive custody plan is not easy, but the

rewards are great. Your negotiated plan, when included in the judge's order, is a legally binding document which will help to shape your family's future. It will be tailored to your individual family needs in a way that one ordered by the judge alone could not. That can help to reduce friction and encourage compliance with the plan. All of you—especially the children—will benefit.

5 ☐ DEVELOPING A FINANCIAL PLAN

A secure financial agreement is important to your children's future. Unfortunately, it can be difficult both to negotiate and to enforce. You may be faced with hard choices, and you'll have to use your own best judgment.

Sadly, you and your children could face real financial hardship once the family is separated. In a major recent study, sociologist Lenore Weitzman discovered that in the *average* divorce, the woman and any children experience a 73 percent drop in standard of living, while the man's standard of living improves by 42 percent.[34] In fact, about a third of all female-headed families with children live in poverty.[35]

With hard work, careful planning, and an understanding of common pitfalls, you'll be better able to protect your children's financial welfare. This chapter is aimed at helping you to do just that. Yet even with the best preparation, you may still find yourself at a disadvantage. Just as there is wage discrimination against women in the workplace,[36] there is financial discrimination against women and children in the divorce courts. While your ideal goal is fairness, your minimum goal must be to avoid dangerous poverty.

Financial negotiation is a major topic in itself, impossible to cover fully here. For that reason, we'll focus in this chapter on only the most common problem areas. If, after reading this chapter, you still have questions and concerns about finances, you may want to consult my book *Child Support: A Complete, Up-to-Date, Authoritative Guide to Collecting Child Support*, which covers all aspects of financial planning, negotiation, and support enforcement.

More immediately, it's helpful to understand and avoid the most common pitfalls that can lead to postdivorce poverty.

CUSTODY BLACKMAIL

Not every bid for custody is sincere. According to Justice Richard Neely of the Supreme Court of Appeals of West Virginia, lawyers commonly use "custody blackmail" to get a better financial settlement for their clients. "Many lawyers representing fathers will encourage a custody bid just to frighten the mother from asserting any financial rights," explains Justice Neely. "They'll say something like: 'My client would like to have custody, but that's negotiable. Now, if the mother will give up the house and the claim for child support, perhaps we can work something out.' Unfortunately, many mothers are so afraid of losing custody, they'll give up anything to avoid a contest."

The problem is serious and appears to be growing. In Professor Weitzman's study, only one man in eight actually sought custody in court—but fully one third used threats to seek custody as a financial bargaining tool.[37]

Custody blackmail might be less dangerous if you knew for certain you were dealing with insincere threats. You could call the father on his bluff, refusing to budge regarding the children's financial needs. Indeed, many lawyers proudly tell stories of doing just that: ". . . So I told the guy, fine, take the kids if you want them so much. Well, wouldn't you know it, in less than a week he'd returned the kids to his wife and was ready to talk business."

The trick may work, but the price is terrible. Children are used as pawns, with their feelings and futures placed at risk. Equally important, there's a risk that the father's custody bid is in fact serious, or could become serious. In that case, you could discover that by following your lawyer's advice, you'd unwittingly given up custody. Your children's future would have been decided on the basis not of their best interests but of a tactical error by your lawyer.

At the same time, the opposite extreme can also be dangerous. Faced with a possible custody challenge, there's a real temptation to panic—to give in to any financial demands, even to give up badly needed support for the children, in hopes of avoiding a custody challenge. This is especially tempting if you think the children would be harmed by a custody fight, or if the father's relationship with the children is poor.

The immediate result, of course, could be poverty or near-poverty for you and your children. That could mean living in a less safe neighborhood, choosing less adequate day care, and perhaps having to work a second job, so that you're spending less time with your children.

Furthermore, by giving in financially to avoid a custody challenge now, you could actually increase your chances of losing custody in the long run. That's because an agreement not to seek custody isn't legally enforceable. Although judges will usually follow the agreement in assigning custody at divorce or separation time, the father could easily come back to court later, saying that circumstances had changed. And with you and the children living in substandard conditions, overburdened by financial problems, a judge might then agree that the wealthier father would make the better custodian.

Every situation is a little different, and you'll have to make the final decision about how firm to stand and how much to give in. Generally, however, it's best to choose—and urge your lawyer to follow—a middle ground. Insist upon settling custody first and money later. Treat the father's custody bid seriously, preparing your case as if it were entirely sincere. Be ready to explain and defend the custody arrangements you think are best for the children. Unless a pattern of past abuse makes father-child contact unsafe, be flexible and open in setting up a custody plan with plenty of visitation.

All this will help defuse the custody issue, making it less open to abuse as a financial bargaining tool. In that context, you can then be firm in negotiating a fairer financial plan.

DIVIDING EARNING POWER

In every state but Texas, alimony is permitted as a way of compensating a parent who is caring for a child, or who has served as the family caregiver and/or homemaker in the past. Yet in recent years, alimony has been under fire. "I don't mind supporting my children," many men say, "but why should I support an able-bodied adult?" Even many women are critical of alimony: "Help for the children is one thing, but I can support myself."

On the surface, this seems to make sense, but it's based on some fundamental misunderstandings. Much as you love your children, raising them is hard work. Traditionally, alimony was a way of partially compensating a woman for the work of raising mutual children. Additionally, since women commonly make career sacrifices in order to raise young children, their earning potential suffers. The father, who is relieved of the job of daily child care, can advance in his career. Alimony can be the way to ensure that if the parents separate, their standards of living stay roughly equal.

Finally, alimony traditionally was also used to supplement low child support levels, for a very simple reason. A father who pays alimony can deduct the payments on his tax form, while child support is not tax-deductible. Thus, to save the father tax costs, courts would set child support artificially low, but make up the difference in alimony.

Today, alimony is so disfavored that it can be difficult to negotiate. That can leave you with only an artificially low child support amount—an amount never intended to reflect the true cost of child raising. This is a major reason that the standard of living of women and children usually drops after a divorce, while the man's improves. In families where the father has been the major wage earner, he keeps the major earning power when the family separates.

There are a number of strategies that can help combat this problem. First, despite the growing prejudice against alimony, it can still sometimes be negotiated. If you are disabled or have spent so many years away from paid employment that your job prospects are quite poor, you may be able to negotiate permanent alimony (to continue until you die or remarry). As Lillian Kozak, CPA and chair of the New York State National Organization for Women (NOW) Task Force on Domestic Relations Law, explains: "It is just as reasonable for a homemaker to receive alimony as it is for a businessman to receive a pension. Alimony is simply a recognition of the social and economic value of homemaking and child raising."

Temporary alimony may also be an option in a wider range of situations. If one or more of your children is quite young or has health problems that require special care, you may be able to show that the child still needs you at home much of the time. During the time you're needed at home, you have a persuasive case for alimony.

Another possibility is temporary alimony geared to help you get education or training you need to reenter the work force. (This is sometimes known by the rather irritating term "rehabilitative alimony," as if homemakers were criminals needing rehabilitation.) Often easier to negotiate than permanent alimony, temporary alimony can help to give you a fresh start.

You may find that any form of alimony is so strongly resisted that it's best to focus only on child support. So long as the child support levels are reasonable, that's fine. In fact, as you'll see below, child support is actually worth more to you in after-tax dollars than alimony. Also, generally speaking, alimony is even harder than child support to collect (because men tend to resist payment more, because judges often take alimony enforcement less seriously, and because some of the best support enforcement laws don't apply to alimony).

There's also an important development in property division law you should consider. Recently, the courts of several states have ruled that a husband's increased earning power should be considered a family asset—to be distributed through property division as well as through alimony. Most often, the cases involve a tangible career asset, such as a doctor's or lawyer's license (earned while the wife worked to support the husband) or a family business (established with the wife's help). In these cases, courts, using expert witnesses, have determined the cash value of the license or business, based on how much it will help the husband to earn in the future. Then the husband has been required to reimburse the wife for her share, either by transferring a large asset (such as the house and/or savings), or by paying installments over time.

Talk with your lawyer about this recent development in the law. Even if your husband isn't a doctor or lawyer, you've probably helped advance his career in many ways. During your time together, you operated as a team, each contributing differently to the family unit. If divorce now leaves him with the greater earning power, it should not leave you behind, in relative poverty. His enhanced earning power is an asset arising from the marriage, and should be shared. Your lawyer should understand that and be ready to advocate on your behalf.

Ideally, any financial plan you negotiate should ensure that both new family units—the one headed by you and the one headed by the father—will enjoy a similar standard of living. That means that if you will be caring for the children, you and they together should have a greater after-tax income than the father alone.

Realistically, few settlements do guarantee the mother and children a standard of living equal to that of the father. If you can negotiate an agreement that gives you and the children together an after-tax income equal to that of the father alone, you've actually done quite well compared to many mothers. Beyond that, your best hope for improving your family's standard of living is to put new energies into developing your career.

TAX EFFECTS

Most divorce settlements have significant tax effects. This means that what looks like a good agreement in before-tax dollars may be a terrible one once you've finished paying

Uncle Sam's share. Because not all attorneys think in terms of long-range tax effects, you need to know the right questions to ask.

First, you should be aware that you will have to pay income tax on any alimony you receive. Your ex-husband, on the other hand, will save money on taxes by deducting the alimony payments.

For example, suppose your total income, including alimony and wages, puts you in a 15 percent tax bracket, while your ex-husband is in a 28 percent tax bracket. If he then pays you $3,000 a year in alimony, this will be the after-tax effect:

BENEFIT TO YOU		COST TO HIM	
$3,000	payment	$3,000	payment
−450	tax cost	−840	tax savings
$2,550	net benefit	$2,160	net cost

If, therefore, in negotiating, your husband says, "I can't afford to spend $3,000 a year in alimony," your lawyer should be prepared to respond, "Yes, but it will actually only cost you $2,160. That's just $180 a month—not much for all the work of child raising."

Child support is different. Because it is for the child's care, and not income to you, it is neither taxable nor tax deductible. Three thousand dollars in child support would be just that—in benefit to your family, and in cost to the father.

Most lawyers know about the tax effects of alimony and child support, but many are less aware of the tax effects of property divisions. According to accountant Lillian Kozak, one commonly overlooked problem in dividing property is the capital gains tax. This is a special tax the IRS imposes whenever property is sold or exchanged at a profit.

Until recently, the capital gains tax on a major asset such as a house had to be paid at divorce time if the asset was transferred from one spouse to the other. Now, due to recent changes in federal tax law,[38] the entire tax will be paid later, when the asset is sold at a profit.

Thus, if your husband offers you your condominium in exchange for other valuable property or rights, you need to be aware that it's a condo with a tax liability. The offer may still be a good one, but you can bargain more sensibly if you know the after-tax value.

Suppose, for example, that the condominium is now worth $80,000, but the original purchase price was only $30,000. Depending upon your tax bracket, you could pay a capital gains tax of as high as $14,000 to the federal government, plus any capital gains tax your state might impose.[39] You would probably have other expenses at that time too, such as a mortgage balance owed to the bank, unpaid property taxes, cost of needed repairs, and real estate sales costs. Thus, by the time you finished paying taxes and other expenses, the "$80,000 condo" might turn out to be worth only half that sum in real dollars.

This is only an example, of course. You can't be expected to calculate the complicated tax effects of a divorce agreement, and you shouldn't attempt it. In fact, many lawyers who regularly handle divorce cases lack the specialized training necessary to evaluate tax consequences. What they do—and what you should ask your lawyer about doing—is to call in a good tax accountant to help determine what you and your husband will each be getting in after-tax dollars. Only then can you be reasonably sure the settlement is a fair one.

HIDDEN INCOME AND ASSETS

Do you really know exactly how much your husband earns? What property he has in his name? Unfortunately, many men hide income or assets at divorce time in order to avoid a fair division.

There are, however, a number of effective ways that an attentive woman and her equally sharp lawyer can detect unreported assets or income. According to Emily S. Bair, an Atlanta attorney specializing in divorce, the common indicators of hidden assets fall into two major categories.

The first is income or assets previously known to exist but that do not appear on current financial statements. Suppose you recall that your husband sold jointly owned GM stock two years ago for about $10,000. Yet an analysis of bank records and other investments for that year shows an increase in worth of only about $6,000. Simple arithmetic indicates that some $4,000 has mysteriously disappeared. While there may be a perfectly innocent explanation, such as taxes paid or unusual expenses, often there is not. At that point, close questioning by your attorney may uncover an undisclosed investment or bank account dating from that time.

A second major indicator of undisclosed assets is unexplained income, however small. For example, suppose your jointly filed 1984 tax return showed interest income of $380. It would be easy enough to assume that that was from your joint bank accounts, but an analysis of those accounts reveals that the interest income that year totaled only $200. That inconspicuous $180 difference could be the key to uncovering an unreported $3,000 passbook account (paying 6 percent interest).

Or suppose your husband is self-employed and reported an income of $25,000 to the IRS last year. Yet deposits to his checking account that year total over $26,000, and you can testify that he brought home an additional $100 per week in cash. That's evidence of $6,000 to $7,000 unreported annual income.

Often the best way to obtain needed family financial documents is to do it yourself. You can get official copies of joint income tax returns for the last six years simply by requesting and returning IRS Form 4506, "Request for Copy of Tax Return." Joint checking and savings account records, if not handy, can be obtained through a personal request to your bank. You should also determine if the bank has any joint or individual loan applications on file, since they tend to list assets fully.

Additionally, are there files at home or in a family business that include such family financial records as stock or money market accounts, personal expense accounts, or business records? The simplest and most direct method of getting copies is to make them yourself, preferably in private and before you separate. That may feel uncomfortable, but family financial papers are your papers too. If your husband doesn't ask your permission to use them, there's really no reason you have to ask his.

Of course, there is another way of getting the financial records: a court-supervised discovery process, with your lawyer requesting them. Unfortunately, it's much more expensive and may be less effective than the self-help method. Important papers have a way of getting lost or even altered as the divorce process progresses, but you can help make sure you've got the full, unedited report.

THE CONDUCT QUESTION

Today, with the advent of "no-fault" divorces, now available in every state, spouses can agree to end a marriage on the grounds that it is irretrievably broken. Unless the issue is separately raised, fault will not enter into either negotiations or any court-ordered property settlement.

If, however, there was serious fault on your husband's part (such as physical abuse, repeated adultery, or desertion), it may be necessary for tactical reasons to plead and be ready to prove fault grounds. Because your husband will probably not want his conduct made public, your willingness to plead fault can act as a powerful bargaining tool. It can also help to explain and bolster a support claim by overcoming any assumption that you deserted the marriage without a good reason.

Great care should be taken in arguing fault grounds, though, for important reasons. First, the truth is that no one is nearly as interested in conduct as the divorcing parties are. What seems like a terrible, shocking slight to an aggrieved spouse will at best excite only mild sympathy in a disinterested judge. And since most judges are still men, they may even be inclined to sympathize with the husband if there's fault on both sides.

Another problem with arguing fault is that high tempers usually lead to high attorney fees. The more tempers flare, the more likely the process is to be bogged down by bull-headed bargaining, unnecessary motions to the court, and so on. In cases like that, everyone loses—except perhaps the lawyers.

Finally, an angry fault contest can quickly turn into an angry custody fight. For this reason alone, it's best to put aside fault claims if possible. Yet if you are seriously disadvantaged in the financial bargaining, or if fault claims are being made against you, pleading and proving fault may be necessary.

It's a delicate question, and one worth some thoughtful discussion with your attorney. Be sure that your attorney understands what fault exists (particularly if it's of a threatening nature, such as physical or sexual abuse). That information is an essential first step in making decisions about conducting your case in a way that will protect both your safety and your financial status.

You should be aware that you may be accused of fault in an attempt to influence the financial negotiations. Once again, you may face a double standard. Behavior such as pursuing a sexual relationship—even, in many cases, once you are already separated and seeking a divorce—may be held against you. Just as an affair or other nontraditional behavior can hurt your chances of negotiating a positive custody plan, it can also hurt in terms of the financial plan. Thus, the value judgments and tactical decisions discussed in Chapter 6 will be important in negotiating a financial plan.

ENFORCING THE FINANCIAL PLAN

If support collection becomes a problem, you'll find that enforcing the law to collect alimony or child support isn't easy. As much as possible, guard against problems *before* they happen.

One useful method is to concentrate as much as possible on assets already in existence. Rather than selling the house and dividing the proceeds, for example, you could agree to lower child support payments in return for keeping the house. That way, you wouldn't have to worry about uprooting the children *or* being totally dependent on child support to pay rent.

In many families, however, there is no large asset such as a house or savings, or the house is too heavily mortgaged to maintain. If the father's wage-earning ability is your greatest family asset, you'll have to depend on some form of continuing support.

In that case, try to get the father to agree to a *voluntary wage assignment*, in which his employer will deduct the appropriate support amount from each paycheck and send it directly to you. (Your court may even have an office where employers send support payments, which are then forwarded to you.) This is an excellent way of ensuring regular payments.

If the father won't agree to a voluntary wage assignment, and gets thirty days or more behind in his payment schedule, you should seek an *involuntary* wage assignment. Under federal law, all states must provide this method for child support collection, and may provide it for alimony collection. If your lawyer doesn't know about this procedure, check with the state office of child support enforcement (see Appendix C). The agency will probably, in any case, charge less for services than your lawyer will.

Once again, the wage assignment process will mean that the employer will deduct and send the support payments— only, in an involuntary assignment, the father can't influence the employer to stop.

It's important to act quickly when nonpayment occurs, before it's allowed to become a habit. The most difficult support enforcement problems are those that have continued unchecked over time. For that reason, be sure to contact your lawyer and insist on effective action at the first sign of nonpayment.

THE DIVORCE-NOW-PAY-LATER PLAN

If your husband has or wants a new lover, he may suggest that you get a divorce decree right away and settle the financial affairs later. In many states, this procedure—called a bifurcated, or two-part, divorce—is perfectly legal.

If you're also eager to get on with your life, it may sound like a good idea. It isn't. Bifurcated divorces have been criticized for unduly favoring what's known in the legal trade as the "financially dominant spouse."

When you think about it, it makes sense. If your husband is anxious to end the marriage and knows that the quickest way to do it is to make a reasonable financial settlement first, he'll be motivated to work toward reaching that settlement. But if he's already divorced, he can drag his feet all he wants.

Even more serious, he could conceivably remarry, perhaps even to a woman with children, before he settles his financial affairs with you. In some states, these new obligations could serve as legal grounds for reducing his ability to pay alimony or child support to you. Even in states where his primary responsibility is technically to his first family, the practical truth is that the existence of the second family will probably affect the distribution of property and support. Either way, your case suffers.

If your husband does suggest a bifurcated divorce, raise these concerns and urge your lawyer to resist if possible. It may increase the time it takes to get divorced, but will probably reduce the time it takes to settle the property.

NEGOTIATING A COMPLETE AGREEMENT

It's important that your divorce or separation agreement be as complete as possible. This will help both to avoid future disagreements and to protect against unexpected losses.

There are a number of major provisions that ordinarily should be included. You'll want to discuss each briefly with your lawyer in advance. They include:

- A clear statement of the *property division.*
- A clear statement of how much, how often, and for how long support will be paid. All amounts should be specifically labeled as to whether they are *alimony or child support,* so that tax treatment and legal effect will be clear. If the children will be living with you most of the time and with their father during vacation times, it should be clearly stated whether any support will be paid during vacation times.
- The agreement should specify who will take the federal income tax *dependency deduction* for the children. (By law, that right goes to their primary caretaker, unless specifically given to the other parent in writing.)
- If possible under your state law, the agreement should include an annual *cost-of-living increase* in any support amounts.
- The agreement should specify who will pay what for *college or technical training.* This is extremely important because, unless there is a specific agreement, a parent cannot be compelled to provide for a child age eighteen or older under the laws of most states. At the same time, because schools expect parents to help pay, your child could be disqualified for financial aid on the basis of the father's income.
- If you expect *other educational costs* for the children before college, such as after-school classes, books, camp, or day care, the agreement should specify who will be responsible for those costs.
- Responsibility for *medical costs,* including health insurance, fees not covered by the insurance, dental costs, and special needs such as orthodontia, should be specified.
- The agreement should state who will be responsible for the payment of which *attorney fees.*
- If there are *debts owed* as a couple, the agreement should state who will be required to pay them.

Other matters that should be briefly noted in the agreement include the following:

- A disclaimer that says you won't be responsible for any *future debts* of your former spouse.
- A provision stating that attorney fees for any *future actions* to enforce the agreement will be paid by the party who violated the agreement. (This protects you against the cost of enforcement if the father fails to support or otherwise live up to the agreement.)
- A statement that *reconciliation* between spouses won't invalidate the agreement. (In most states, a single act of intercourse may be considered reconciliation, and you don't want to be seduced into giving up your rights under the agreement).
- A warranty that there has been *full disclosure* of all income and assets of the parties. (This helps you to re-open the case later if you discover that major assets were hidden from you.)
- A mutual *covenant to execute documents* necessary to put the agreement into effect (such as property deeds, stock transfers, insurance assignments, etc.).
- A mutual *waiver of inheritance rights* not specifically reserved in the agreement.
- A statement that the signing of the agreement is *voluntary and knowledgeable,* in that both parties understand it and are not under duress to sign.

As you review your divorce or separation agreement before signing, think carefully about the terms. Ask yourself the following questions:

- Is each provision clearly stated so that no one could misunderstand its meaning?
- Is it a provision I can live with financially and emotionally?
- Do I really understand the agreement fully, including its long-range practical, financial, and tax effects?

- Is the total effect of the agreement fair and reasonable?

If you can answer yes to all these questions, congratulate yourself on a job well done. Your success in putting together a solid agreement will be a help to your family for years to come.

6 | CUSTODY AND SOCIAL CONTROL

As you and the children's father negotiate a custody plan, your ability to bargain will depend in part upon how strong your case looks. If the father wants custody and believes the judge will grant it to him, he'll have little motivation to compromise. He may even persist to court.

The best defense against this problem is to be prepared with a strong custody case, as if you were ready to go to court tomorrow. This means guarding against criticisms or perceived weaknesses in your case. It may also mean presenting yourself in a manner likely to impress the average judge.

Most judges make a real effort to set aside their personal prejudices when they hear a case, and to truly focus on the needs of the child. That's part of their job, and many do it remarkably well.

Unfortunately, some judges can be quite critical if a woman doesn't fit their idea of how a "good woman" should behave. Many are middle-aged men who have enjoyed the privileges of power and leadership. A world in which women live independently from men, raising children in nontraditional settings or with nontraditional values, can seem alarming to them. It's not how they were raised. It's not an idea they'd like their wives to consider. And it's certainly not a concept they want to encourage or reward.

Even if your life seems fairly tame to you, it's possible that a judge wouldn't agree. Consider that until fairly recently, there was really only one socially acceptable lifestyle for a woman with children. She should be married. (Widowhood created the one limited exception: A widow could remarry after a suitable mourning period, or stay "wedded" to the memory of her deceased husband.) As a married woman, she should put homemaking before career, and duty before passion.

Today, of course, few judges are shocked or offended by the mere idea of a divorced woman. Some can also accept a woman who is nontraditional in other ways: a woman who works in a job with long hours or that has been traditionally held by men, who is not religious, who lives in an apartment instead of a house in the suburbs, or who is sexually active. A few can even accept a *really* nontraditional woman, who chooses another woman as her sexual partner, is involved in political organizing, occasionally smokes marijuana, or teaches her children to think and challenge rather than to blindly obey.

Many, however, cannot. They would rather see children raised in a traditional home than in a less traditional one. Particularly if the father is remarried, or has a housekeeper or his own mother who can provide child care, the judge may be inclined to see the father's new household as more suitable.

In the examples that follow, we'll look at possible ways to prepare a strong custody case in the eyes of even a critical judge. Your first and most crucial task will be to show exactly what your role and responsibility for child raising has been. This is important because many judges assume that if a woman doesn't fit their idea of a traditional mother, she's probably an uninvolved mother.

Also, because most judges are themselves unfamiliar with child care responsibilities, they often don't understand just how much work is involved. If they learn that the father has even one task he regularly does, such as preparing breakfasts or putting a child to bed, this can reinforce their idea that the mother is not particularly involved. Reasoning that such a "modern" mother probably spends only an hour or two daily on child care, the judge may conclude that the father's half hour equals half the responsibility.

For that reason, you'll need to be prepared to document your true role with the children. You can begin by writing down the crucial facts about your children's early years. Did you take time off from work to care for an infant child? Did you breast feed? Who did the regular care: changing diapers, bathing, tending to the child at night, and so on? Make a list of specific contributions you've made over the years.

It's also helpful to begin immediately keeping a diary that briefly notes all the activities you now do for or with the children each day. Include everything—making meals, talking with teachers, helping with homework, bedtime talks, and so on. There's no need to describe all this in detail; just be consistent and complete. One month of brief notes ("Fixed breakfast, drove Debbie to school . . .") is better than two days of flowery prose. Bring a copy to your lawyer's office at the first visit.

There are other ways your lawyer can help you to prove your parental role, and we'll examine these in later chapters. From the beginning, however, the diary is something very important, which you can and should do yourself.

Even if a woman can show that she's been the children's primary caretaker, there are a number of lifestyle factors that could be used to try to undermine her custody case. Some are choices on her part, while others are necessities of life. Nonetheless, if a woman is employed outside the home, has never been married, is sexually active, or has had sexual experiences with other women, any of these facts may be used against her.

You need to be prepared to consider and answer these types of charges, no matter how ridiculous they seem to you. Only then can you hope to put aside social control issues and focus on the true priority: a custody plan that will serve your children's needs.

Of course, all other things being equal, it is probably easier to raise a child if you're independently wealthy and don't need a job, if you're at least formerly married, if you have no social life, and if you are heterosexual rather than homosexual. If nothing else, the world around you is more supportive. Children can also be conformists themselves, worrying if others will reject them for having an unusual home life. Yet, while these concerns are all valid, they are certainly not the only or even the most important factors in deciding custody.

We'll try, then, to put various lifestyles into perspective, looking at ways to guard against unfair criticism. Because nontraditional families also face social and personal challenges, we'll explore ideas for meeting those needs too.

Many of the suggestions that follow involve value judgments. Simply stated, you are least likely to lose custody if you can convince a judge that you are extremely traditional and respectable, sexually chaste, a perfect but now abandoned wife, and a doting mother who is constantly available to her children. Yet those may not be your ideals—for example, you may feel that your strong points are creativity and adventurousness. To try to fit someone else's picture of perfection could make you feel (and perhaps seem) false and wooden. You may also hope to be a trendsetter, to open up a judge's mind to the values of your more modern style of parenting.

Only you can decide what's right for you. To a certain degree, you can emphasize those features of your lifestyle that are likely to impress a judge, while deemphasizing the less conventional. It's the kind of selective honesty you probably use frequently in life. You present yourself one way during a job interview, differently at a crowded social event, and still differently with old friends.

Selective honesty, however, doesn't and shouldn't mean dishonesty. You might be discreet about a sexual relationship, but that's different than denying it exists. If you deny it and are later proved to have lied, you'll be judged not only for the relationship but also for the lie. Although a lie is very tempting when you know that an honest answer (or even silence) will probably be unfairly used against you, the chances are that being caught in a lie will hurt you even more.

In a very general way, this chapter offers basic ideas about what commonly impresses judges deciding custody. How closely you'll want to follow the ideas is very much a personal decision. To help you decide, you'll probably want to discuss them with your lawyer. Ultimately, however, the choices must be yours.

THE BUSY WORKING MOTHER

It almost seems silly to list this as a lifestyle choice. With today's low child support levels (and alimony almost unknown), what divorced or divorcing woman can afford *not* to be employed? Yet employed mothers are able to spend less time with their children, and that fact is sometimes used against them in custody disputes.

Your first defense against this tactic will be to demonstrate your daily involvement with the children, as noted above. Additionally, it may be helpful to be ready to demonstrate (1) that you work out of financial need and (2) that you've made suitable child care arrangements.

To show that you work out of financial need should not be difficult. You'll be making up a budget of necessary expenses anyway, for use in financial negotiations. On a separate sheet of paper, write down all nonemployment income available to you and the children, including any child support or alimony now being paid. The gap will, of course, be obvious.

You may enjoy your job, and may resent having to justify it. No one, you may rightly note, is questioning your husband for having a job. Nonetheless, since there is a double standard, most women find it's best to have the figures ready. That way, if the issue comes up in negotiation, your lawyer can say, "It's clear that both parents need to be employed. Let's move on to more important issues."

To demonstrate the second point, suitable child care arrangements, you first have to establish them. It isn't easy, particularly if the divorce is pushing you into the work force suddenly. Yet it's very important, not only for the immediate safety of your children but also to avoid a really strong custody challenge. Women have lost custody for even temporarily leaving younger school-age children home alone.

This is a point on which you should marshal every bit of help you can get—from family, friends, and community resources. Your state social services department may be able to refer you to both day care centers and family day care (individuals who care for a few children in the home) in your area. Your child's school may know of after-school activity programs. Friends and family may be able to provide baby-sitting.

If divorce finances are pushing you into the work world before you've had a chance to make child care arrangements, try not to jump too quickly. Talk to your lawyer about the urgency of temporary child support. You may also want to consider AFDC (Aid to Families with Dependent Children) and/or food stamps to tide you over until you can start work. Although AFDC payments are too low to present a long-term solution, they can provide help in an emergency. The associated social service department may also offer job placement or help finding child care, although the quality of these programs varies widely by state and community.

NEVER-MARRIED MOTHERS

If you were never married to your child's father, there is very little chance that he'll challenge you for custody. The much more common problem among never-married families is a father who just disappears.

Yet occasionally it does happen that a never-married father will seek custody of his child. The process for doing this is fairly similar to the divorce and custody process. First, however, paternity (the fact that he really is the father) must be either acknowledged (admitted by both parents) or established (proved by a court process, usually using blood tests). Since this is also the first step to collecting child support, it's sometimes done long before there is any custody conflict. (For a more complete explanation, see the chapter on establishing paternity in my book *Child Support.*)

Once paternity is established or acknowledged, the laws regarding custody are the same or similar in most states, whether or not the parents have ever been married. Again, however, judges' attitudes often make the difference.

Custody contests in this setting are a good example of how traditional assumptions can sometimes work against anyone—male or female—who doesn't play by society's rules. A judge faced with a never-married mother might consider her (but, by the classic double standard, not the father) sexually "loose," and might therefore be prejudiced against her. On the other hand, the judge might assume that the father refused to marry the mother, was disinterested in family life, and would thus not make a good parent. In either case, the judge would be depending on stereotypes, not on individual parent-child relationships.

If you find these assumptions distasteful, they are. Your best bet is to understand them and guard against them, but not to try to take advantage of those assumptions that seem to favor you. The minute you or your lawyer tries to argue your case based on one traditional assumption in your favor, you'll find it that much harder to argue against all the traditional assumptions that can be used against you.

Instead, stick to the facts. Are you really the one who has cared for the child since birth? If so, concentrate on showing that. Did the father fail to visit or pay child support when you really needed help, but suddenly express interest in custody when you got a new boyfriend? Show that too.

The old prejudice against unmarried mothers as "loose women" is pretty much gone today. Just the same, to be safe, you might put some extra effort into presenting yourself as a very respectable, responsible person by dressing conservatively for court appearances. If there's a reason you didn't get married, you could briefly explain it. If you have a family priest, minister, or other community figure who could be a witness for you, that might also be helpful.

SEXUAL ACTIVITY

It is utterly normal and natural that, once divorced, you should want a social life. For a healthy adult, that probably also means a sex life. Unfortunately, it can spell custody problems down the road. If a judge hears that your children are waking up to unknown faces at the breakfast table, it could weigh heavily against you.

Some women decide not to plunge too quickly into postdivorce dating. Such restraint can be wise. It can give you time to heal from the divorce, and give your children time to adjust to all the divorce changes.

When you do start dating, it's best to be discreet. Even young children are a lot more aware of your affairs than you may realize. Most children also have strong emotional reactions to the people their parents date. They may be angry and confused, feeling threatened by a man they imagine is replacing their father. (The sooner after the breakup the new man enters the picture, the more likely and the stronger this response may be.) Or they may cling to him in their loneliness for their father, only to be disappointed if it's just a fleeting friendship.

It's a good idea, if you can, to schedule casual dates to begin and end while the children are off doing something else. Thus, for example, if the children see their father from ten in the morning to eight at night on Saturday, try to arrange a picnic date for noon. It's a pleasant, low-key way to get to know someone new, and spares your children the strain of meeting everyone you date. You can also, if you want, have wild, passionate sex all afternoon, without risk of upsetting anyone.

Once a relationship is established, you'll probably want your children and your new friend to meet. (Actually, your children will probably demand a meeting once they figure out from phone calls and chance comments that something's up.) Generally, an informal, child-centered outing such as a visit to a park or the zoo is a good setting. If the children do express anxiety, let them talk about it and try to reassure them.

The more difficult question is whether or when you should invite your friend to share your bed while the children are at home. To that, there's no easy answer. By rights, it's your home and your private life. Yet the truth is that no matter how long you wait or how delicately you handle it, it may not look good if you're challenged for custody. With each new relationship, it looks worse. It also, quite honestly, can be stressful and confusing for children. You'll have to give careful thought to all the factors: how important it is to you, how it might affect the children, how likely you think a custody challenge actually is, and what risks you're willing to take.

Possibly you'll even be asked at some point to agree never to have a lover spend the night as a condition of keeping custody. It may be that the children's father truly worries about the situation upsetting the children. Or it may be that as your ex-husband, the idea of someone else in "his" bed with you upsets him. Agreeing to that condition could mean avoiding a custody fight, or it could just open the door to more and more demands to control your behavior. Again, you'll have to trust your gut instinct for what seems right.

Incidentally, don't even consider having a lover stay with you and asking the children to keep it secret from their father. If you can't keep the matter private, don't expect that they can. Even if they mean well, they'll forget or slip. They'll also be confused by the secrecy and feel caught in the middle. Finally, as we'll see in Chapter 7, secrecy can be a dangerous habit to teach children. All in all, it's best not to do anything in front of your children (even teenagers) that you're not willing to have published in the local newspaper.

SEXUAL EXPERIENCES WITH OTHER WOMEN

All the difficulties and challenges of postdivorce dating increase when your partner of choice is a woman. Homophobia—fear of homosexuality—is deeply ingrained in our culture, and many judges share the fear. Additionally, you're never allowed the option available to heterosexual couples: to make your union "respectable" by marrying your partner. No matter how stable and committed your relationship is, it can be very difficult to convince a judge that it offers long-term stability to your children.

One decision you'll have to make is how open to be about your sexual feelings and experiences. An advantage of openness is that you don't have to live in fear that someone will "find you out." It can also be a way of expressing pride and comfort with who you are. Unfortunately, too much openness too soon can create problems at home. It can also open the door to a custody challenge.

To a certain degree, your amount of openness will depend on your lifestyle and may change over time. You may, for example, have occasional sexual experiences with other women, perhaps to explore longings or curiosity you've felt for a long time. That may or may not mean that you'll eventually choose a woman as a long-term partner. If you can keep these early experiences private, you'll avoid a great deal of possible confusion and criticism. It's much like the choice that many women make to keep first dates with men private—but with higher stakes.

Yet if a deeper relationship develops, there may come a point when it's impossible—or just doesn't feel right—to keep your lover and your children apart. In fact, many divorced mothers who develop a committed relationship with another woman want to share that relationship with their children. It can be a good idea. Just as children can benefit from a parent's remarriage to a loving, welcoming spouse, they can enjoy a parent's loving, welcoming same-sex partner.

That's not to suggest, however, that the transition is easy or without significant risks. You should be aware that even if you are careful and responsible, and even if the children respond well to the new relationship, you still could lose custody if challenged. So being open—"coming out"—is clearly a big decision.

If you do decide to involve your partner in your family life, it's essential to be sensitive to your children's needs and emotional reactions. They will probably have some of the emotional responses they would to any new partner—nervousness, rejection, perhaps anger, or perhaps clingy dependence. They may also react to the fact that you and your partner are the same sex. Younger children may simply be confused if they've only known heterosexual couples in the past. Older children may worry that friends will be shocked and will reject them. Teenagers may also become anxious about their own sexuality.

It's helpful if you let the children get to know your partner as a friend first. That doesn't mean denying the nature of the relationship—just don't push the sexual issue. Then, as they notice your closeness and begin to ask questions, you can turn it into a discussion rather than an announcement.

As much as possible, give your children an opportunity to talk about their feelings, listen to them carefully, and then offer honest answers and emotional support. You might even think about whether short-term family counseling or child counseling would be beneficial in sorting through the feelings and making a good start. That good start will help improve your family life, as well as prove a strength if custody is later challenged.

Once the children know, it probably won't be long before their father knows (at least if they're in contact with him). While some men are not shocked by a lesbian relationship, others are and want to "protect" their children by seeking custody. Some feel insulted and angry that a woman they once loved now prefers a woman. Commonly, these two sets of feelings—honest concern and hurt pride—get mixed up together, so that the man argues ardently that the children will be hurt by the relationship, not realizing that he's really the one who's upset.

There's no right strategy about telling or not telling the children's father. "I'm sure my ex-husband knows we're lesbians," says one woman, who lives with her lover and her children, "but he doesn't ask and I don't tell him. I think if I said it right out, he'd feel he had to do something about it. It would almost be like a challenge to him. As it is, I think he'd rather not know officially."

Another woman, who became concerned when her ex-husband began questioning the children about her roommate/lover, wanted the children to be out of the middle. Although it was difficult for her, she made a lunch date with her ex-husband and told him honestly about the relationship. Fortunately, he'd already met the partner when picking up the children, so he didn't have to imagine her as someone awful. He was still upset by the news, but talking about it directly seemed to help him to be calmer.

Your children will probably have questions about how to talk or not talk about the relationship themselves—not only to their father but to friends and acquaintances. It's helpful to explain to them that you are proud and happy about the relationship, but that some people in our society don't understand when two women love each other. For that reason, you don't tell everyone. If someone asks you and you don't want to talk about it, you don't lie; you just tell them it's private.

If, in that conversation, you want to explain that you prefer not to tell their father because it might upset him, that's fine. But again, you really can't expect or ask children to keep your secrets. The best you can do is to let them know that if *they* want to keep the information private from their father, that's okay. Make it very clear, however, that "privacy" doesn't include lying.

If the children's father does decide to seek custody, there's a real danger that concern and prejudices about lesbianism will dominate the proceedings. As much as possible, you'll want to redirect the focus to the more important issues of quality and continuity of parenting.

Before you can do that, however, you may need to defuse the sexual issue. One good way to do this is to look for a mental health expert who is informed and sympathetic about lesbian parenting. Testimony from someone like this can help you if you go to court, as well as give you stronger bargaining power in negotiations. A lawyer with experience in lesbian custody cases may know of suitable experts, or you can check with local gay rights groups or with national groups listed in Appendix B.

No matter how persuasive your expert, the prejudices against lesbians will not entirely disappear. A common strategy that seems to help is to present a fairly "straight" image. If you dress in a skirt and a stylish jacket, set your hair and wear makeup to court, it won't make you a better mother—

but it will probably increase your chances of keeping custody. Similarly, inviting your children to participate in a gay pride march with you may help them to feel good about their family life, but it could also shock and offend a judge who hears about it later.

You may be asked to promise not to live with your lover or allow her to spend time with the children. This is, of course, a terrible restriction on your family life, particularly if yours is a committed, long-term relationship. If you agree, it may increase your chances of winning custody, at least in the short term. Whether or not you are willing to make such a promise, however, is a very personal choice. If you don't think you can live with it, it's best not to say you will. If the judge grants you custody on the condition that your lover never spend the night, you stand a high chance of later losing custody if you regularly break the condition.

Interestingly, some judges are actually more favorable toward lesbian mothers if there is a long-term live-in partner. Although they might prefer a more conventional stepparent, they reason that at least the children won't be exposed to a series of new lovers. Your lawyer may know the records of local judges on this issue and be able to help strategize. It could even be helpful, in some cases, to bring your partner in as a witness to talk about her role in the family. She could create a positive impression, helping to overcome negative stereotypes about lesbian relationships.

Because custody challenges to lesbians can be so serious, there are specialized guides for mothers and lawyers involved in these cases. To locate them, see Appendix A.

It's unfortunate that when you make nontraditional choices for your family you'll be judged by a traditional system. Often the safest way to defend against custody loss is to play by the traditional rules. It may feel uncomfortably like saying, "Well, yes, I admit I'm a lesbian [or sexually active outside marriage, or involved in a career], but in every other respect I'm a good mother."

You may feel that you're a good mother *including* the aspect in question. You may want to help redefine what it means to be a good mother, to show that being a good mother includes being strong and independent and honest about one's true self. It's true that such redefinition is needed, and that each mother who is frank about her lifestyle choices helps to educate those around her, perhaps paving the way for mothers and children who follow. At the same time, it's important to balance that desire for social change against the immediate risk of losing custody. To do that, you may want to strive for an honest—but guarded—presentation of your case.

7 | PROTECTING AGAINST DANGER AND INTIMIDATION

It wasn't easy for Denise Grant to sit down with her husband and tell him she wanted a divorce. She was afraid of his temper. Still, talking it out seemed like the right thing to do.

When she told him, he threw a glass against the wall. Then another. Then, though she cried and tried to stop him, he stormed off in the car with their four-year-old son, Jeremy.

He came back about 3:00 A.M., put Jeremy into bed, and went to bed himself. Before he fell asleep, he said one thing to Denise: "Next time, I'll take the kid for good."

Physical violence, sexual molestation of children, and paternal kidnapping are all shockingly common in our society today. The extreme cases that come to our attention are only the tip of the iceberg. For every husband who beats his wife, there are more who threaten. For every father who sexually abuses his daughter, there are more who watch and control their daughters with an intense sexual jealousy. Sometimes a spirit of intimidation can exist even before the violence is tangible.

If you're living in an atmosphere of intimidation, you need to know what protections are available to you and your children. Otherwise, you're limited not only by what's happening now but by your fears for the future. "What will he do next if he gets more angry?" you may think. "I'd better agree to whatever he suggests so things don't get worse."

Unfortunately, that reaction can be dangerous in itself. It can make you agree, against your better judgment, to a custody plan harmful to the children. It can force you to give up financial rights that you and the children can't afford to lose. It can also reward violent and threatening behavior, so that your husband is actually *more* likely to use it in future conflicts.

A better approach is to plan ahead, hoping for the best, as you prepare for the worst. Learn now about protecting against abusive behavior, including your options when the legal system doesn't offer the protection it should. Prevention is especially important in protecting against child sexual abuse and paternal kidnapping.

Sometimes it's hard even to believe that abuse is really happening, much less to consider that it could get worse. Such a reaction is normal, because family violence and sexual abuse are so painful and shocking. They are a betrayal and a violation by someone who claims to love your mutual children, and whom you once loved and thought loved you. It's only natural to be torn by wishful thinking that perhaps the violence will go away on its own. It's also natural to want it to stop but to be hesitant—out of fear or out of love—to do anything that might hurt the abuser.

Sadly, abusive behavior doesn't go away on its own, and you can't make it go away with heartfelt pleas or an appeal to fairness. You can, however, take positive action to protect yourself and your children from it.

There's a common myth that men who abuse do so because of their wives' faults. Thus, a man's sexual abuse of his children is blamed on his "frigid" wife, a batterer is thought to beat his wife because she "drives him crazy with her nagging," and a man who kidnaps his children is believed to do so because "she wouldn't let him see the kids."

This kind of thinking blames the victim while accepting the abuser's excuses as if they were acceptable reasons. Even if every sexual abuser had a sexually unresponsive wife, every batterer had a nagging wife, and every kidnapper had a wife who interfered with visitation (assumptions that are not supported by any evidence)—would even that excuse or explain the abuse?

It wouldn't, because it overlooks the basic question of *why the abuser chooses a violent response to the situation.* A nonabusive man faced with sexual difficulties in a relationship would either work on solving them with his partner, accept the fact of a lukewarm sex life, or seek a new adult partner. A nonviolent man with a nagging wife would make a similar choice to improve, accept, or end the relationship. A nonviolent man faced with visitation problems would try to work them out personally or seek court enforcement. Only an already violent or abusive man would try to resolve his problems by hurting others.

It is perhaps true that, in a very deep sense, men who abuse do so because they feel incapable or inadequate to express their feelings in a less harmful way. Like most criminals (and family violence *is* criminal), many abusers have had rough lives. That, however, is a problem that you didn't cause, can't control, and can't cure. Your first priority must be to protect yourself and your children from violence and abuse.

The most basic fact to understand is that even violent people don't behave violently just because they're angry. With very few exceptions, they do so because they are angry *and* they think they can get away with it.

"Abusers are very aware of who's in power and what will or will not be stopped or punished," explains David Adams of EMERGE, a counseling service for male batterers in Boston. "For example, the man who flies into a violent rage over burnt toast at home will probably not blow up at a police officer who gives him a speeding ticket. He may be angry— far angrier than he was over the toast—but, eyeing the officer's badge and gun, he'll probably nod and respond politely."

PREVENTION STRATEGY

Your basic prevention strategy will involve some combination of three factors:

> • Encouraging your children to discuss their concerns and fears with you, so you can help protect them.
> • Preventing opportunities for abuse, either by safeguards on visitation or, if necessary, by total lack of contact with the abuser.

- Making it clear that any abuse attempted will be quickly prevented or punished.

Within that basic framework, you'll make many individual decisions about what's right for your family.

Because our legal system often denies that abuse exists, while it strongly protects a man's "rights" as "head of the family," abuse prevention is often difficult. Fortunately, most cities (and many smaller communities) now have battered-women's service networks, rape crisis centers, and/or sexual abuse prevention programs. National networks also exist to help find missing children.

Appendix C at the end of this book has a listing of national organizations that can help you. Most likely, however, your local resources will be most important. Don't wait for an emergency to occur before you start learning about these community resources. Right now, put down this book and pick up a phone. Find out:

- Where you can get services if you're battered, and what services are available.
- Whether there is a rape crisis center, and whether it also handles child sexual abuse.
- What hospital or clinic is recommended by rape crisis advocates if you are raped.
- What hospital, clinic, or treatment program is recommended by those advocates in case of child sexual abuse.

Make a list of emergency phone numbers and keep them near your phone. Consider, too, whether there are services you can use now. Battered women's programs in particular are excellent resources for providing emotional support, helping you to sort through your options, offering concrete services, and putting you in touch with professionals who can help protect you. If you feel afraid, threatened, or harassed (as well as if you've actually been beaten or had your children threatened), you qualify for those services.

As you ask for help and emotional support, you are

drawing upon and finding your own inner strength. That inner strength—which has already helped you to begin building a new, independent life—will also help you to care for and protect your children during a difficult time.

Another important strength will develop as you talk with your children about ways to stay safe. In *The Safe Child Book,* educator Sheryll Kerns Kraizer describes an excellent method called the "What if . . ." game, designed to reassure rather than frighten. It's a question-and-answer-game you can start with ordinary kid-type questions like: "What if the dog chewed up your library book? What would you do?" Gradually, you can introduce more serious questions.

Encourage your children to take the lead and think up their own "What if . . ." questions. They'll find it fun, but also a good way to explore their own fears. You may find, in fact, that their fears match yours. If you let your children bring up fears in their own way, rather than introducing yours, it will be more reassuring and more informative to you both.

"What if," your daughter might say, anxious about her father's possessiveness of her and angry criticisms of you, "Dad wouldn't let me come home anymore?"

"Well, you could call me on the phone, couldn't you? Then I'd come get you."

"But what if he said I couldn't call?"

"Well, you could wait and call when he was at work, couldn't you? Or you could ask an adult like a teacher to help you, and keep trying until you found one who would help."

"But, Mom," your child might persist, "what if you didn't come?"

At that point, you might ask, "Why do you think I wouldn't come?" If your daughter is afraid that her father would stop you, you could explain that you could get a judge to help. If she's afraid that you'd be angry or are tired of her (which many children fear during a divorce), you can explain how much you love her and that you'd always want her home. In other words, you'll be responding *now* to precisely the fears that could otherwise later prevent your child from taking protective action.

While it's good to let your children ask most of the "What if . . ." questions, you can also ask some of your own. It's important, though, to ask gentle, general questions, not ones that present scary ideas they've never considered. For example, sometimes fathers who abduct their children tell them that their mother is dead or doesn't want them anymore, so that the children won't try to contact her. But to say, "What if Daddy told you I was dead?" would be frightening and harmful in itself. Instead, you could say, "What if someone you really liked told you something bad had happened to me, but you weren't sure if it was true? Would you just believe them, or would you try to find out for yourself?"

You should also ask the very important "What if you were doing something you're not supposed to do and something bad happened to you?" and then emphasize that the children would still be protected, not punished. Often children are afraid to contact a parent during a frightening experience because they know they've broken a family rule.

PREVENTING PATERNAL KIDNAPPING

As a parent, you've probably told your children, "Never go with strangers." Did you know, however, that they are far more likely to be kidnapped by their father than by any stranger?[40]

Paternal kidnappings are extremely harmful to children, and can be difficult to prevent. Assuming that your children's father is not an obvious danger to them, you can't legally or morally tell them, "Never go with your father." You can, however, plan ways to keep them as safe as possible.

An important defense against paternal kidnapping is your children's ability to get in touch with you. With coaching and practice, even a four-year-old can learn to use the phone and memorize your phone number. Children love to make phone calls, so you can make it a game. Ask your baby-sitter or family members to help by encouraging your child to call you from their homes. Whenever they do call, respond happily, so they'll be encouraged. You and the baby-sitter can set limits on how often they call, but some repetition is important to help them memorize.

Of course, you'll want them to know how to reach you from out of state and how to get operator assistance. Since children enjoy gathering facts about themselves, you can practice with a quiz game when you're driving in the car or doing chores. "What's our phone number for long-distance collect calls?" "What town and state do we live in?" "What's my full name?" (Many children know their mothers simply as "Mommy.")

While you prepare your children with information that would help them locate you, you should also prepare a special file with information to help locate them. It should include clear, recent photos of each child, as well as medical, dental, and school records.

Also keep a file with identifying and location information on the father. In addition to photographs, you should have his social security number (very important), addresses of friends and relatives, present and former employers, any credit card numbers or other financial information you have about him, and a list of clubs, interests, and organizations.

Be sure to keep both files in a very safe place where neither the father nor your children have access to it. You don't want the location information to disappear with the children.

Most of this information gathering can be done quietly, without your children even noticing. If you discuss it at all, do so in a light, encouraging way, saying, "This is great, because if you're ever far away and I don't know where you are, this will help us find each other." Since children worry about getting lost anyway, you'll be reassuring them, not introducing a new fear into their minds.

If you think there's a real danger of paternal kidnapping, it's a good idea to set some ground rules for your children. The idea is not to frighten them or warn them of possible abduction, but simply to create a safe structure. Kraizer recommends that you tell your children this:

"Dad and I are having some problems getting along, but

we don't want you to be caught in the middle, so we're going to have some ground rules.

"First, I'll always tell you ahead of time when Dad's going to pick you up. If he should come when we weren't expecting him, don't go with him until you've talked to me first, no matter what he says. If you can't reach me, just stay where you are until you do.

"Second, Dad and I have agreed he won't be taking you on any overnight trips. If for some reason he does take you on an overnight trip, you should call me right away, no matter what time it is or where you are."

After you explain, ask your children to explain it back to you, so you'll be sure they understand. If they ask the reason for the rule, just explain that it's important for parents and children who live together to each always know where the other is.

You'll also want to explore your protections through the legal system. While a court order isn't perfect protection, the absence of one can increase the danger. That's because, in most states, if you and your husband are separated but have no court orders, either one of you can legally take the children anywhere. If your husband runs off with the children, you may be able to get some reluctant police help in finding them, but probably not immediate help in getting them returned.

If you have a court award of at least temporary custody, however, you'll find it easier to get help when you need it. Another possible protection is a court order stating that the noncustodial parent cannot leave the state with the children. A third option is restrictions on overnight visitation. Any of these provisions can be made in an order after a temporary custody hearing or, in most states, after an emergency protective hearing. That's good, because you won't have to wait a long time.

(A word about the restriction on leaving the state: Most judges insist that the provision limit both parents, at least until there's proof that only one parent is creating the danger. If this is a problem for you, because you fear you may have to flee the state because of violence or abuse, be sure to discuss your concern with your lawyer in advance.)

Once you have your order, keep the original safely tucked away in the information files on father and children. You should also have certified copies made at the courthouse to give to school officials or day care providers, with the strict instructions that the children not be released to their father. Make sure that school officials know they should contact the police and show the order if they have trouble preventing the father from taking a child.

Finally, you can help protect against child snatching by keeping careful track of where your children are at all times. Make sure that they know where they should go after school, as well as who will be picking them up after any event. Your vigilance will be an important part of your children's safety.

IN CASE OF CHILD SNATCHING

If, despite all your efforts, father and children disappear, you'll need to act fast. You should work closely with your lawyer, but your ideas and resourcefulness are crucial. The following checklist should help you to organize.

Court Order

Do you have a court order giving you temporary custody? If not, your lawyer should immediately seek an emergency order.

Police Assistance

Interference with a valid custody order is a crime. Violating a protective order by taking the children would also be a crime. In some states, fleeing with the children even before there is any order is a crime. By seeking an arrest warrant for the crime committed, you can get police help in apprehending the children's father and having the children returned to you. (You can decide after they are returned whether you want to continue to press charges.)

Depending on your state law, you may be able to get the state prosecutor to issue a felony warrant, the more serious class of crime. Since it is a federal crime to flee to another state to avoid a felony warrant, this would allow the Federal Bureau of Investigation to join the search.

Your lawyer can assist you in getting the police, the prosecutor, and the FBI to cooperate. Although technically there is no requirement for a citizen to have a lawyer to get police or FBI help, the truth is it will probably speed things along.

In Appendix D, you'll find a listing of parental kidnapping and child custody jurisdiction laws for every state. Bring it to your lawyer's office, so that the lawyer will be ready to show the police what laws have been violated by the kidnapping. You and your lawyer should press for the most serious charge possible to maximize police and FBI involvement.

Detective Work

A good private detective, if you can afford one, can focus more time on your case than police or federal investigators will. Be sure that the detective is reputable, however, because a few unscrupulous detectives are actually known to collaborate with kidnapping fathers and inform them of progress in the search.

Friends and Family

Some of your husband's relatives or friends may know where he's gone or at least know how to reach him in case of emergency. They may be willing to consider helping. Speak to them personally, emphasizing your concern for the children and your desire to work out any problems with the father.

Keep in mind that they may have heard terrible things about you, and be guarded at first. Try to be patient and reassuring, no matter how angry you feel. It could be your best hope for finding the children.

Former Employer

Your husband may have left an address with his former employer for sending a last paycheck or year-end tax form. The employer may also be contacted later for job references as your husband applies for work in a new location.

Post Office

The post office may have a forwarding address, which you can obtain by submitting a simple request form.

Moving Company

If a car or van was rented for the move, local rental agencies may have records indicating the city where it was returned. If movers were hired they may have records of the new address. Agencies can be called and asked to check their records.

Financial Records

- If traveler's checks were purchased, the issuer's records should show where they were later cashed.
- Bank account records should show any change of address or interbank transfer, as well as where checks were cashed.
- Credit card records indicate where credit purchases were made.
- A credit union, which usually requires a request in advance to receive funds, may have a forwarding address.
- If the father owes money, he may continue to make loan payments from a new location.
- If he seeks a new credit card, the local credit reporting agency may receive a request for a credit report.
- There may be continuing contact with a life, health, home, or auto insurance company, with records showing payment of premiums or filing of claims.

Motor Vehicle

Your state motor vehicle department (or that of another state, where you think the father might be) may have driver's license, car registration, and insurance information indicating a new address. However, they will notify the father that they have sent that information to you.

In the New City

If you think you know what city the father is in, you may be able to locate him through utility companies. Customer service offices of local gas, electric, and phone companies will generally tell you if they have an account in a customer's name and at what address. You should also, of course, check the current phone book for that city, especially as time passes. (Nationwide phone books are available at major libraries.)

Professional Groups

Labor unions or professional associations (such as lawyer, architect, doctor, accountant, or teacher licensing boards) are another generally available source of home and work address information.

College and Trade School Records

If the father is a graduate of a college or trade school, its alumni association or placement office might have his current address, especially if transcripts were requested for job applications.

Hobbies

Even hobbies can be the key to finding address information. Bowling leagues, athletic clubs, civic organizations—whatever your husband has participated in previously and might take up in a new city—are all worth contacting.

Children's Records

If the children are enrolled in a new school, their old school may be asked to send records. Similarly, new health care providers may request past health records. Ask your child's school and clinic to notify you of any request.

Parent Locator Service

The federal and state Parent Locator Services are valuable resources, offering computer access to a wide range of public records using social security numbers. While you cannot get this information yourself, the police, the judge, or the state prosecutor can.

Missing Children Services

The National Center for Missing and Exploited Children is the best known of several organizations that provide information and assistance to aid you in locating your child. They offer several excellent booklets, free of charge, to help you protect your children against kidnapping or other abuse. Additionally, they can send you an up-to-date listing of local groups that provide practical and emotional help. See Appendices A and C for the address and available publications.

PREVENTING THE PHYSICAL OR SEXUAL ABUSE OF YOUR CHILDREN

Child abuse, like child kidnapping, is a harmful and frightening abuse of parental power. According to Judith Herman, a psychiatrist and the author of *Father-Daughter Incest* (Harvard University Press, 1981), child abuse is most likely to occur in a family where the father has a strong need to control and exert power over other family members—through threats, violence, favoritism, and/or mood swings. Because children are frightened by their father's erratic behavior and especially fear losing his love, they try extra hard to please him. In many cases, that frightened effort to please may include submitting to sexual abuse or keeping quiet about physical or sexual abuse.

An essential part of protecting your children against abuse is to help them understand a simple fact: They don't have to cooperate with adult behavior that frightens them. As in kidnapping prevention, that doesn't mean alarming them with detailed warnings about possible future dangers. Instead, make sure they know that if something bad does happen, they can get help.

You can help prepare your children by (1) encouraging them to trust their own instincts when a situation seems odd, frightening, or upsetting; (2) letting them know that they'll still be loved if they say no to adults who make requests that frighten them; (3) encouraging them to talk with you about these situations; and (4) letting them know that you'll help protect them.

For several reasons, it makes more sense to give your child the freedom to report what's upsetting, rather than establishing specific rules like: "Tell me if your father ever hits you" or "Tell me if your father touches you inside your underpants." First, if these things have so far never happened, it could scare your child just to hear about them, creating an idea of the world as an unsafe place. Second, children have very literal minds, and abuse that occurs later might not fit your description. To try to describe all possibilities of abuse— hitting, kicking, sexual fondling, pornographic pictures, exhibiting of genitals, and so on—would surely confuse and terrify your child. A much more helpful approach is to simply explain, "You can always tell me about anything that happens to you, no matter what it was or who did it, and even if someone told you not to tell."

A common misunderstanding about sexual abuse is that children may be abused but not realize something bad is happening, so they won't talk about it. In fact, even very young children who are sexually abused—like those who are physically or emotionally abused—definitely know that something is happening that feels upsetting and scary. Often, their own instincts will tell them that a certain kind of touching or affection doesn't feel right, long before it ever progresses to overt, identifiable abuse.

Yet children may be especially afraid to speak up if they've been taught to obey and try to please adults (including the adult who's abusing them). Frequently, they are tricked or persuaded to "keep it our secret," or they fear punishment or family problems if the abuse is discovered. They may also be unsure whether anyone will believe or act on their concerns.

There are lots of little ways that you can let your children know they don't have to obey or protect adults who are frightening them. Suppose that a friend or relative visits who wants to kiss your son in greeting. He says no. Your saying, "Honey, Aunt Debbie loves you and came a long way to visit. Can't you give her a kiss?" tells him, that Aunt Debbie's feelings are more important than his right to privacy. If, later, he's worried because his father wants to take baths with him, how does he know you won't urge him to go along with that? It's better to risk hurting Aunt Debbie's feelings than to give your child the impression that his feelings and fears aren't important to you.

To emphasize this concept, you can also use the "What if . . ." game described above. "What if," you might say, "your teacher told you to cut holes in your dress and use it for an art project?" If your daughter laughs and says, "I wouldn't do that!" congratulate her for good thinking. If she says, "I guess I'd have to," you can reply, "No, you could tell her no and if she got mad, you could come home and tell me. Then I'd go talk with her and tell her we don't cut up dresses." You haven't frightened your child, but you've told her she won't be punished for using her own judgment if a trusted adult suggests something that seems wrong.

You can also use the game to explore specific dangers, but only in general, nonthreatening ways. For example, you wouldn't want to frighten your child with: "What if a man pulled down your pants?" but you could say, "What if an adult you *did* like tried to touch you in a way you *didn't* like?" then encourage answers like: "I'd say 'Cut it out!' "

and "I'd tell you so you could make them stop."

Sheryll Kraizer and other experts on abuse also suggest a family policy of "No secrets." Tell your children this:

"Secrets are when older people ask you to not tell things they do. You don't have to keep secrets. You can tell the adult, 'No, we don't keep secrets in our family.' Or, if the adult makes you promise not to tell, it's okay to tell me anyway. Adults shouldn't make children keep secrets, so it's the adult who's breaking a rule, not you for telling.

"Surprises are different—that's when you don't tell something good that's going to happen. Privacy is different, too—that's when you decide it feels good not to tell something. Surprises and privacy are okay, because they help make you feel happy."

Of course, once you make this rule, it's important to keep it yourself. You can't expect your child to distinguish between "Don't tell Daddy that Jim sleeps in my bed" and "Don't tell Mommy that you sleep in my bed."

It's also important to avoid telling your child who is "safe." Except for yourself, you really don't know. Once you thought their father was safe; now you may be less sure. Over time, you may consider a future husband or other relatives or friends safe. It's still not right to label them for your child.

That doesn't mean you should distrust these people or burden your children with fears and warnings. Just don't stand in the way of your children's protective instincts by labeling *anyone* safe. You may mean: "I have faith that X won't hurt you," but your child hears: "Don't tell me if X upsets you."

Since children may be afraid to talk directly about abuse, it helps to be aware of signs of distress, and to ask what's the matter. For example, if your child seems very frightened to go off alone with an adult, it's important to ask her privately why she's afraid. If she seems nervous and secretive, that's worth asking about too.

Sometimes, through unusual sex play with other children, children act out abuse that's happening to them. "All children play doctor," explains Kraizer. "Normally, this involves mutual and healthy exploration and play between children. It does not involve one child victimizing another, nor does it include contact between the mouth and the genitals, or attempts to penetrate the vagina or the anus."

If you discover your child engaging in suspicious, even alarming sex play, try to react calmly. Kraizer suggests direct, nonthreatening questions, such as: "What game are you playing?" "Who else plays this game with you?" "What happens when you play this game?" Often, children will tell you exactly where they learned the "game," and you'll know if there's a problem.

If you want more help in talking with your child about this topic, you might call a local abuse prevention or rape crisis service, and see if there's a counselor who can answer your questions.

WHAT TO DO IF YOU OR YOUR CHILD IS ABUSED

If abuse occurs, you'll have two priorities: (1) treatment of the injury (physical and psychological) and (2) prevention of future abuse. Both are crucial whether it is physical or sexual abuse of your child, or battering or rape of you.

Immediate medical treatment is a must whenever there is any pain, any physical sign of abuse such as cuts or bruises, or any reason to believe that sexual abuse has recently occurred. Don't wait for obvious physical problems before seeking treatment, since there may be injury to parts of the body that you can't see (particularly in the case of sexual abuse). Also, the medical report will be important evidence to help you document the abuse and protect against it in the future.

A mental health exam is also important, particularly if it's your child who has been battered or abused. A specially trained psychiatrist, psychologist, or social worker will talk with your child, document any evidence of abuse based on that conversation, and help arrange therapy to counteract the trauma. If your child doesn't appear to need immediate medical care (that is, in the case of delayed discovery of abuse), a prompt psychological exam is most important.

In case of rape or child sexual abuse, many doctors and other medical personnel aren't equipped to effectively and sensitively offer the services you need. They may understand little about the nature of sexual abuse and may also lack specialized technology for documenting abuse.

Fortunately, many hospitals or larger clinics have special units equipped to document and treat sexual abuse. Services may include specially trained medical personnel, technology designed to preserve physical evidence (often known as "rape kits"), and mental health professionals trained to talk with children about abuse. In a few programs, hidden videotape cameras record a child's conversation with the interviewer, sparing the child the need to repeat her or his story again and again.

If, as suggested in the beginning of this chapter, you've checked out local resources in advance, you'll know immediately where to go in an emergency. This is important in avoiding a risk such as sending your child to a hospital that reports there is no sign of sexual abuse—when a better-equipped clinic would have detected ample evidence of abuse. (Yet if you do need emergency services and don't know where to turn, call your telephone operator and ask for rape crisis services.)

"The importance of a prompt, competent, reliable initial evaluation can't be overstated," says psychiatrist Judith Herman. "Children are often afraid to talk about being abused. If they get a negative reaction the first time they try, or they aren't quickly protected, they may later clam up or retract their report. Also, if there's physical evidence, it could be gone by the time you get to a better-equipped clinic or a better-trained doctor."

This is a real problem, explains Herman, because there's no shortage of mental health professionals who will interview the father (without ever speaking to the child) and then inform the judge that the father is "not the type" to abuse a child. To guard against this, you need the strongest possible professional documentation of the abuse.

Additionally, wherever you take your child to be examined, the doctor and/or mental health workers will be legally required to report the abuse to your state child protection agency. According to Herman, not all such agencies do a good job of documenting abuse. Again, to offset any possibility of a poor response from the child protection agency, you need the best possible initial report.

Some women, concerned about the abuse-reporting requirements, or concerned that the exam might frighten the child, don't take the child to be examined at all. While understandable, this is a real mistake. Your child needs help if abuse has occurred—and you need evidence to protect your child against future abuse.

Another crucial step will be to make certain that your lawyer is experienced in handling cases involving abuse. Many lawyers are not. If your lawyer isn't, check with your local battered women or rape crisis program for a referral to one who is, or check with your state bar association referral office.

Work closely with your lawyer in documenting any type of abuse to you or your children. Where there are physical injuries, such as bruises or cuts, some women take or have a friend take photographs. Instant cameras, if available, are best, because then you know if the pictures are coming out all right. To indicate the date, the current daily newspaper can be included in the photo.

Any witnesses and a diary of events are also helpful. If it's your child who has been abused, check with teachers to see if they've noticed anything suspicious.

POLICE PROTECTION

Anytime you or your children are in immediate physical danger, you may need police protection. It is a crime in every state to hit or beat another person, or to sexually molest a child, whether or not the abuser is a family member. Your family is entitled to police protection from battering and abuse, if necessary by having the abuser arrested and removed from the home.

Studies show that the police action most effective in preventing future violence is an immediate arrest.[41] Even if the abuser is soon released on bail, the arrest delivers a strong message that violent behavior is not allowed and carries serious penalties.

It is not, however, always possible to have a batterer arrested on the spot. One reason is a limitation on police arrest powers. Hitting or beating alone (battery) and threatening to hit or beat (assault) are classified among the less serious crimes (misdemeanors). Generally, a police officer cannot arrest for a misdemeanor unless it is committed in his or her presence. Since a beating generally stops when the police come to the door, an arrest may not result.

Assault or battery with a weapon or with the intent to kill or rape is classified as a more serious crime (a felony). In most states, the weapon need not be a gun or a knife; it could be anything likely to injure someone, such as a table fork, a telephone receiver, or a book. A few states will even consider a strong man's fists a weapon, so that it would be a felony for him to strike with his fists.

An officer can arrest—and in fact has a legal duty to arrest—whenever there is "probable cause" to believe a felony has been committed. Probable cause means just what it sounds like: that there's cause to believe it probably happened. So if you explain to the officer that your husband beat you with his fists and his shoe—and you're obviously bruised or cut—the officer would have probable cause to make an arrest.

It is also a crime to sexually abuse a child, but an immediate call to the police can be a problem. A sexual abuse case is difficult to document, and the average cop on the beat won't be able to make an on-the-spot decision about arresting. Also, it could increase your child's sense of fear to have a police officer come to the house after the abuse to investigate. A much better route is to take the child first for the medical and mental health exam.

For both battering and child sexual abuse, you may want to consider a long-term remedy through the criminal justice system. In some areas, local prosecutors' offices have special units for these crimes. The goal is not necessarily to put the abuser in jail but to prevent future abuse.

In an effective program, the abuser will be convicted or, fearing conviction, plead guilty, and will then be given a suspended sentence. As long as he meets certain stated conditions—for example, does not further harm you or the children, helps to financially support the children, and perhaps attends counseling sessions for abusers—he will stay out of jail. He may never spend a night behind bars, but the knowledge that he could helps keep his behavior peaceable.

Ideally, a system offering immediate short-term arrest when violence occurs, followed by the threat of longer-term jail if abuse continues, is the best hope for preventing future abuse with minimum disruption to the family. Yet the reality often falls short of the ideal. In many areas, due to old stereotypes about family violence not being "real" violence, battering cases are not pursued vigorously. Police may refuse to arrest, or prosecutors may fail to prosecute. In the worst cases, individual police or prosecutors (who may be abusers themselves) actually blame the women for the problem.

Prosecutors' offices vary widely in their ability to handle child sexual abuse cases effectively. Some are very sophisticated and sensitive, offering special child advocates to interview your child, and innovations such as hidden videotape machines to record the interview. Most prosecutors at least take the cases seriously and do try hard.

In one respect, the criminal justice system offers an advantage over the traditional family law system. In the family law setting, people are used to thinking in terms like: "There are two sides to every story," "People say all kinds of things during a divorce," and so on. This can feed right into denial about violence against women and children. Yet police, prosecutors, investigators, and criminal court judges are all very aware that some people are just plain violent and dishonest. They've probably seen some very violent criminals who make very convincing witnesses, and they are less likely to be fooled.

Once there's a conviction, criminal justice officials are also less likely to worry about the father's paternal "rights" to unlimited access to his victimized children. That conviction will also be important if the father ever seeks custody, because it's strong, clear proof of past abuse.

Your local battered women's center, rape crisis center, or the counselor who treats your child for sexual abuse can probably give you tips about your area police and criminal justice system. Since many programs are improving rapidly, be sure the information you get is up-to-date.

PROTECTIVE ORDERS

In many states you can now get extended police and court protection even without (or before) seeking a criminal conviction, and without (or before) seeking a divorce. The remedy is through protective orders, which may be available even if you and the abuser have never been married. Details vary slightly by state, but here's a general idea of how they work. (For information specific to your area, ask your attorney or a battered women's service group.)

To get a protective order, you would fill out a simple petition at the court assigned to hear such cases. You would then go before a judge to testify about the violence and abuse occurring against you or the children. Your lawyer should be there with you, although legally a lawyer is not required. Any proof you have, such as medical reports or photographs of bruises, you would show to the judge. If you have witnesses to bring, that's good too.

The judge, after hearing your evidence, would have the power to issue a temporary order to protect you. The order might be quite limited (perhaps merely ordering the abuser to refrain from hitting, threatening, or harassing you or the children) or more extensive (for example, ordering the abuser to leave the family home, and ordering the police or sheriff to arrest and hold him while you have the locks changed).

Note that this hearing, unlike most other kinds of legal hearings, is one-sided (ex parte). You're there, but the person you're complaining about (the defendant) isn't. This is because it's an emergency. The defendant will have his chance to answer, however. Within a week or two, a second hearing will be set, and both of you will have a chance to come in and be heard. *Be sure to attend this second hearing with your lawyer.* Generally, the emergency order lasts only until the second hearing, and if you're not there to describe the violence and ask for an extension of the order, you'll lose your protection.

What exactly does a protective order do for you? First, it shows the abuser you're serious about stopping the abuse, and will take legal action if necessary. In some cases, it can give you immediate police assistance in getting an abuser to leave the family home or in leaving with the children yourself. It also lets the abuser know that his actions are not permitted by the legal authorities and that, in effect, he's being watched.

Your having a protective order may also give the police extra arrest powers if the order is later violated. Here's why. As you just learned, it's a general rule that police can't arrest for a simple assault or battery unless it occurred in their presence. In most states with protective order laws, however, the police have a duty to arrest if there's probable cause to believe a protective order has been violated. This is true even if the offense would not otherwise be considered a felony, and even if it wasn't committed in the officer's presence.

Protective orders are often helpful in child sexual abuse cases. Because of difficulty of proof, however, you should discuss this and other options with your lawyer.

In some states, protective orders may contain provisions for temporary custody of the children and for temporary alimony and/or child support.

SUPERVISED VISITATION

If there are positive aspects to the relationship between the children and their father, you may be wondering whether visitation will be possible, and if it's a good idea. Once again, that's a big decision, and you'll probably want help in thinking it through. A lot will depend on how severe the abuse was, how long ago it happened, whether the father has sought counseling or other help, and how the children themselves feel.

Possibly you won't be allowed to choose whether there will be visitation. Many judges feel very strongly about the importance of maintaining the father-child relationship, even where there's a history of abuse.

Whether you favor visitation or face a judge who insists on it, you'll want to seek a visitation plan that is as safe as possible. Your lawyer can help you work out exact details, but it may be helpful to know about some possible options. Most are not safe in the case of a currently violent man, but can aid in maintaining a sense of structure and control with one who, although abusive in the past, shows a willingness to avoid abusive behavior now.

You might, for example, agree to brief daytime visits in public areas only, such as a playground or park near your home. If you have family in the area, perhaps arrangements could be made for the father to visit the children at your parents' or other relatives' house. Visitation at his parent's house is not a good protection, since they may not believe he's potentially abusive and may do little to supervise.

Every state has a social service department assigned to protect children from abuse, and you could enlist their aid in supervising visitation. If they agree there's a need, the services will probably be free. They may also provide free or low-cost counseling if needed.

You should understand that the social service agency will function primarily to serve and protect the children. Thus, if you and they have different opinions about what's right for the children, they're likely to follow their judgment rather than yours. They might also report their opinions—about the children, and about both parents—to the judge. This can be a problem, because some workers tend to minimize the danger of violence, and may view you as "overreacting" when you are appropriately concerned. For this reason, it's important to try to stay calm in dealing with these workers.

If you've sought help through a criminal justice prosecution, departmental agents may be more helpful in structuring and supervising visitation. They have a power the social service agency does not: the ability to immediately punish wrongdoing against you or the children.

Long visits, overnight visits, leaving the state with the children, or visiting the children while intoxicated all should be specifically prohibited in the court order if possible. If you need to keep your location secret, ask to set up a safe, supervised place where you or someone else can drop off and pick up the children when they see their father. Returning home with the children, you should take special care to be sure you're not being followed.

Obviously, there are many factors to consider before agreeing to any supervised visitation plan. It's no panacea, even when the father is reasonably cooperative. If he's actively resistant to the plan, it could spell future danger. Yet for some families it makes sense as a way to maintain what's good in a parent-child bond, while guarding against what's bad.

KEEPING YOUR LOCATION SECRET

If the violence against you or the children has been severe, you may wish to consider leaving secretly and concealing your new location. This option, although not right for every family, has allowed many battered women and their children to begin a new, safer life.

Most medium or large-sized cities, and even some smaller communities, have emergency protective shelters for women and children escaping from family violence and abuse. The shelters tend to be crowded but friendly, with dedicated staffers who understand (and often have been in) situations like your own. They can help you to find housing and a job if necessary, as well as ease the transition for you and the children by offering emotional support and counseling. Shelter locations are kept secret for your protection, but their phone numbers are listed in the phone book. Most shelters are free or very low-cost to families in need.

You should know that many shelters struggle with problems of inadequate funding and are often filled to capacity. If you call a shelter and it's filled, ask where else you might call, and keep trying. If you're thinking about moving out of state, you could ask your local shelter to help you make contact with shelters in the new community.

In some respects, fleeing can be the safest choice. If successful, it means that you and your children won't have to face the daily abuse, threats, and risks that continued contact with an abuser can bring. It can mean a fresh start.

Yet the risks are substantial. Although you know you are fleeing to protect the children, others might not see it that way. If their father later finds you, he might be more likely than before to run off with the children himself or to legally seek custody. If you can't then prove that you fled in response to serious danger, your risk of losing custody would be serious. Depending on the state where you live, it's even possible that you could face criminal prosecution for child kidnapping.

Once again, we're talking here about protecting against the worst danger, which may well never happen. In fact, many women who flee from abusers with their children find that after an initial period of outrage, the father never really looks for them. Yet since others find that the abuser searches diligently and desperately, it's wise to be prepared. This is especially true if he is wealthy enough to be able easily to launch a full-scale search and custody battle.

For this reason, it is crucial that you fully discuss the possible consequences with an attorney experienced in abuse cases *before* you flee the state or hide permanently. Of course, you may be in immediate danger and have to flee without advance planning. One way to handle this problem is to seek temporary refuge at a local protective shelter for battered women, then ask their help in referring you to a good lawyer before transferring to an out-of-state shelter. Try to put together as complete a plan for where you'll go and what you'll do as possible.

Wherever you go, don't tell anyone outside the shelter your new address if you can avoid it. Even your lawyer should know only your general plans and your telephone number.

If you don't already have a custody case pending in your home state, your lawyer can help you to decide whether it's best to start one immediately or to wait and open the case in the new state. If there is a case pending in your home state, your lawyer should stay involved, trying to help you to get and defend a permanent custody order. You, in turn, should stay in close touch with your lawyer.

If you already have temporary or permanent custody, your lawyer should show the order to local police, federal prosecutors, the Parent Locator Service, and the private nonprofit child locator services, in order to try to block any agency cooperation in a search for you. Possibly, your lawyer will be able to give you a sense of whether and how serious a search is being made.

If a search for you is under way or threatened, you'll have the strain of living under cover. You may have to begin using a different last name, and avoid having past school and medical records forwarded.

If you think the Parent Locator Service might be used to locate you, be aware that they'll eventually pick up any use you make of your social security number, such as on the job, in applying for AFDC, or in getting a new driver's license. The safest (but most inconvenient) route is to work "under the table" and to walk or use public transportation. Another possibility is to get a post office box, so that if the locator service learns where you work, at least it won't learn where you live. Some women will also make a slight error (such as reversing two digits) in their social security number on forms that require it and hope the error isn't discovered for some time.

Ultimately, what kind of protection you seek—whether to flee, seek help from the criminal justice system, or try to structure supervised visitation in a divorce decree—is a decision only you can make. A great deal will depend on your own family dynamics: whether the violence is frequent or occasional, how severe it is, how much the children are affected, and whether there are any positive aspects to the father-child relationship worth trying to salvage. It will also depend on what you learn about the effectiveness of court and law enforcement protection in your area.

You can also combine more than one method into a total plan that fits your family needs. For example, you might move to another state but not keep your location secret, seeking sole custody with strictly limited visitation. Due to the distance, much of that visitation might be carried out through the much safer medium of the mail and phone calls.

Perhaps the only really helpful rule of thumb is to follow as vigorously and completely as possible whatever course of action you choose. If you decide to hide, hide effectively—don't stay with a friend down the street and let the children play out front. If you have provisions in a divorce agreement designed to protect the children during visitation, consult your lawyer at the very first violation. And if you get a protective order that says your abusive husband will be arrested if he tries to enter your home, call the police if he's jimmying the front door lock.

Although there are no easy answers, there are successful ones. Millions of women have emerged from abusive situations and gone on to build a new life for themselves and their children. With energy, effort, and the help of others, you can too.

8 | WHEN NEGOTIATION FAILS

Sometimes, negotiation doesn't seem to work. You may prepare and plan carefully, and your lawyer may advocate skillfully—yet you can't reach an agreement that you feel meets the children's needs. Perhaps joint custody doesn't seem to be an option, either because you'll be living too far apart or because you feel it would be too disruptive to the children's lives. You believe that you should have custody of the children, while their father says he should. The issue seems non-negotiable.

At that point, you have two options: You can agree to give up sole custody or you can prepare to argue your case in court. In the right situation, each can be an honorable, even a wise, choice—and each can be painful and difficult.

The most obvious advantage to persisting in court is that you may succeed in keeping custody. If you have been the children's primary caregiver, you know that it's important to your children's emotional well-being to preserve that relationship. If, additionally, the father-child relationship is poor or potentially abusive, you may feel that you have a duty to resist the father's custody bid.

You may also want your children to know that you care enough to fight for their custody. In a larger sense, you may want to resist a system that undervalues relationships and overvalues money and power. All these are important concerns.

At the same time, the court process for determining custody can be extremely hard both on children and on parents. Until the final decision is made (which could take as much as a year or more in most states), children often feel anxious, caught in the middle, unsure of their future. Even afterward, they may feel worried and even guilty about their role in the conflict. These, too, are important concerns, although you can help your children deal with the stress by being sensitive to their needs and feelings.

Another factor is money, since presenting and defending a custody case in court can be very expensive. Some women find that even if they are successful in gaining permanent custody, their ability to care for the children will be badly hurt by the extra legal expenses. Sadly, some can't afford to persist at all.

Finally, of course, you could go through the difficulty and expense of a court contest and lose. Painful as it is to consider, that possibility must be factored into your decision.

Some women decide to give up custody as an act of love. They may want to continue raising the children—who they feel would benefit by their mother's care—but they also believe that a court battle would hurt the children too much. Like the loving mother in the King Solomon story, who agrees to give up her baby rather than allow the child to be cut in half, these mothers agree to let go. They sacrifice their daily life with the child, but spare the child the pain of being caught in the middle.

You may find that your decision is complicated by your own strong, even overwhelming, emotions as you face the custody process. Deep anxiety and fear are normal, but you can avoid panic as you begin to plan and take action. Anger ("I'll show him—he'll never get custody!") and despair ("I might as well give up. I failed at marriage, and now I'm failing with the children") are also quite normal, but try to be aware of them and not let them rule your decision-making. Your focus should be on what you think will be best for the children.

A final key factor will be your state's custody law and the policies of local courts. This can affect your chances of obtaining custody through court action, as well as how harrowing and expensive the court process is likely to be. While all states officially decide custody based upon the "best interests of the child," variations in local law and policy can influence the result.

If, for example, you live in a state that gives top consideration to who has been the children's primary caretaker in the past, you are much more likely to have custody granted to you by a judge. Additionally, because any inquiry will be limited to the factual question of who's done the child raising in the past (rather than the more judgmental question of who's been the "better" parent), it will probably be a much quicker, less expensive, and less painful process.

As of mid-1986, the only state offering a "primary caretaker presumption"—that is, a rule that the child's past primary caretaker, if not unfit, shall be presumed to be the custodian best for the child—was West Virginia. Several other states, however, appear to formally or informally make use of a preference in favor of continuing custody with the past primary caretaker.

At the other extreme are states that have an official presumption or preference in favor of joint custody. In these states, unless there are unusual reasons that your children will be particularly harmed by joint custody, a judge would probably decide in favor of it. The mere fact that the father has not been involved in child raising in the past, combined with the recommendations of the mental health authorities discussed in Chapter Four, would probably not succeed in convincing a judge to grant sole custody under these state policies. A history of child abuse or family violence, however, would probably be considered cause to avoid an order of joint custody in most states.

As of mid-1986, Florida, New Hampshire, Idaho, and Louisiana all had laws requiring a legal presumption in favor of joint custody, while several other states had laws or policies favoring joint custody awards. In other states, where there are no official preferences or presumptions to guide a judge in deciding what's best for the child, it will be left entirely to the judge's discretion. For some judges, that will mean choosing the parent who appears to offer the "best" home life, while others will opt for the most experienced parent.

Since custody law and policy have recently been in a great deal of flux, you should ask your lawyer about local law and policies and how they may affect your case. In this chapter, we'll simply look at how the court process typically works so that you can maximize your chances within it. Keep in mind that you and your lawyer will be continuing to negotiate even as the court process progresses, so you may not have to go through the entire process.

Because each case is different, no one can tell you when it's best to give in and when to persist. This chapter, combined with consultation with your lawyer, will give you information about your options. Your friends, a support group, and/or a therapist can give valuable emotional support. Your decision, however, must be your own.

Once you've followed a course of action, don't torture yourself wondering whether you could have done it differently. There isn't a single right way to solve this problem. Just do the best you can, whatever you choose—and give yourself credit for doing so.

SEEKING A COURT CUSTODY ORDER

Sometimes, when negotiation fails, it can make you doubt the strength of your own case. "If I've got a good case for custody," you may think, "why isn't their father just agreeing to it? Does he know something I don't know?"

In fact, negotiation can fail for any of a number of reasons. The children's father may be refusing to agree out of confidence and commitment to a goal, but it also could be overconfidence, blind anger, the hope that you'll give in without going to court or that you'll make financial concessions. He could even be following the (possibly bad) advice of a lawyer who hopes to inflate the legal costs. So while it's fine to consider and discuss with your lawyer any weaknesses in your case, you don't have to let a divorcing spouse's opinion define your own.

In earlier chapters, we've talked about developing a

strong case for negotiation. The same factors and strategy that strengthened your case in that context also strengthen it in the court process. Your daily role as primary caregiver, your work to establish as stable a lifestyle as possible amid change, your close relationship with the children—all these will help to show a judge that the children will benefit by your continued caring for them. The only difference is that now, in addition to asserting the importance of these factors, you and your lawyer will have the task of proving them.

There are four basic steps to the court custody process: the temporary order, the custody investigation, the custody hearing, and the permanent (or final) order. We'll examine each of these steps, as well as the process for appealing an order to a higher court and the process for modifying a custody order later.

THE TEMPORARY ORDER

This is the court order that says who will have custody of the children until the judge makes a final decision. Usually, other matters are also included in the order, such as temporary child support, who will be allowed to live in the house, and what property must not be sold or what funds spent until the property division is complete.

The temporary order is usually issued quickly, because it is the court's way of establishing control over the case (thus discouraging child snatching or the hiding away of shared assets). It also protects the children by providing for their immediate care and support. Commonly, the temporary order will be issued at the first scheduled court hearing, at an emergency protective hearing, or even at an informal meeting between the judge and the lawyers in the judge's office.

Perhaps because the temporary order is issued so quickly, its importance is often underrated. Yet consider that it will probably determine where the children will live over the next several months. (Although the temporary order can be changed at any time by the judge, it rarely is, because judges like both to save their own time and to avoid constant disruption to the children.)

Having temporary custody improves your chances of being awarded permanent custody, for two reasons. First, judges recognize that a change in custody between the temporary and the permanent plan will be disruptive to the children. Second, if you've been the primary caregiver, temporary custody emphasizes that fact (while temporary custody in the father could make the judge doubt or disregard your long-term primary role).

The fact that temporary custody is decided so quickly can work in your favor. Usually, rather than delve deeply into the facts of the case, the judge grants temporary custody to the parent who is already caring for the children at that time.

If you've been caring for the children, it's essential that you not disrupt that pattern even briefly before the temporary custody award. For example, suppose that immediately after learning that your husband wanted a divorce you left the family home, returned to your parents' home, and began looking for an apartment for you and the children. If you left the children with their father, he might within days get an order giving him temporary custody of the children and temporary possession of the family home, simply by convincing a judge that this would help stabilize the children's lives. A year later, that temporary order could become a permanent one.

Note that the temporary order may also, as in this example, affect the use and possession of the family home. While a home isn't quite as essential to a child's stability as the parent-child relationship, it is important. It's where the children are used to sleeping, eating, entertaining their friends, and generally living their lives.

If you can stay in the home with the children in the short term, you maintain some stability during a difficult time. You also increase the chances of negotiating the continued use of the family home. Just as temporarily leaving the children can lead to permanent loss of their custody, temporarily leaving the home can lead to permanent loss of its use and possession.

This is a commonly recognized fact among lawyers,

which means that the children's father, if he has a lawyer, has probably heard it. It is not unusual for a stubborn contest to develop, with each spouse wanting the other to leave. If this happens, ask your lawyer to push for a prompt hearing to decide who may stay in the house.

In the meantime, the atmosphere at home can get unpleasant. Ask for an emergency protective hearing *if and only if* violence or abuse is occurring or is seriously threatened. If there's no overt abuse, but you feel you must leave to protect the children from a tense, unhealthy atmosphere, be sure to take the children with you and continue to push for a quick resolution to the problem. Since the decision to leave the house is one with serious practical consequences, it's wise, if you can, to consult with your lawyer beforehand.

Occasionally a father, hoping to get a temporary order in his favor, will physically evict the mother from the family home, change the locks to keep her out, and then go to court seeking a temporary order of custody and temporary possession of the family home. Of course, he doesn't appear in court and admit what he's done; instead, he reports that the mother has deserted and, claiming that he doesn't know her whereabouts, asks for an emergency one-sided hearing.

If this happens to you, be prepared to act quickly. Contact your lawyer, your local battered women's services, and the police. Ideally, they'll help you get back in and the threatening father out. At a minimum, they'll be your witnesses that your "desertion" wasn't voluntary.

A somewhat more delicate issue occurs if the father leaves with the children before there is a temporary order. Legally, he has just as much right to do this as you do. In that case, your best remedy is to urge your lawyer to press for a quick hearing to determine temporary custody. If you act quickly, there's less chance that the judge will decide the children are settled with their father and grant custody to him.

The more hotly temporary custody is contested, the more involved the temporary hearing is likely to become. Possibly, it could include proof and argument about matters such as who is the primary caretaker and who can offer the children the best home life, much as the permanent custody hearing eventually will.

It's helpful if you and your lawyer are prepared to offer evidence and arguments about your care of the children at the temporary hearing. Since you will definitely have to offer that evidence at the permanent custody hearing, however, we'll explore the evidence process in that section.

THE CUSTODY INVESTIGATION

Shortly after the temporary custody order is issued, the court may order a custody investigation. Its purpose is to learn more about the home, habits, and environment offered by each parent to the child or children. It is conducted outside court, in a less formal, more personal setting.

Practices differ by state or even by county within a state. In some areas, custody investigations are quite in-depth, and are conducted by a mental health professional who talks at length with family members in their homes. Occasionally, neighbors or friends may be interviewed, but generally only those whom one or both parents suggest. Other investigations may be limited to one or two brief meetings in which each parent is interviewed by a court employee.

Ordinarily, the investigation will center upon—but may not be limited to—questions about the children and their care. While many investigators simply look to see who is already active and involved as a parent, others try to judge who would be the "better" parent according to some abstract ideal they hold.

It's natural to feel anxious about the interviews, but you don't have to be intimidated. You'll probably find that as you begin to talk about your children, you'll relax and project a good image as a caring mother. Obviously, you have strong reasons for believing the children will benefit from your continued care. Those positive qualities will shine through as you talk.

At the same time, just as you might prepare for an important job interview, it often helps to prepare for the custody interview. A good way to start is to discuss with your lawyer the type of questions frequently asked in your area. Practice answering them, either with your lawyer or with a friend, so you'll feel more confident with your replies.

Try to plan a relaxed schedule for the day of the interview and the evening before, and eat regular meals. Don't drink any alcohol or take unnecessary medications. If you think it will help, arrange to talk on the phone with a friend just before the interview. Leave plenty of time to get to the interview, so you'll be on time and arrive relatively unharried.

If the interview will be held in your home, be sure the house is clean and orderly, including any play area or child's room. If the walls look bare, tape children's drawings to them. If you can't afford children's books, borrow some from the library and leave them in view. Be sure, if the children will be at home during the interview, that they are clean and suitably dressed, and that they have activities to entertain them while you're talking.

Most interviewers limit their questions to matters reasonably related to child raising. Some, however, ask intrusive, unrelated questions—about sexual preference and experience, past drug use, and political views, for example—which could prejudice a judge against you. This can be a real problem, particularly because your lawyer isn't there during the interview to object to inappropriate questions.

There is no single right way to handle this problem if it occurs. In some situations, an honest (but carefully worded) answer is the best. It can win you respect for your honesty, and may even give you a chance to explain matters that the children's father plans to prove and use against you. Yet there are risks. One woman who lived in a conservative area frankly admitted that she had tried marijuana in college. Later, in an order granting custody to the father, the judge relied heavily on that minor fact.

Knowing how unfairly small admissions can be used, there's a real temptation to lie. Quite aside from any moral question, however, lying can be at least as risky. You could get caught in a lie, either because later you give an inconsistent answer or because the truth is proved later by other evidence. Even if you're not actually caught, a skilled interviewer may notice your nervous glance or tone of voice, and may doubt your answer. Any perception of you as less than honest will probably hurt you.

Sometimes it's possible to avoid a problem by answering a question as narrowly as possible. For example, one woman who was asked, "Do you smoke marijuana?" didn't want to discuss the fact that she had in the past. She answered, quite honestly, "I'm a mother raising two children with very little help. I don't have time to go to a movie, much less to go out and smoke marijuana."

A good option in difficult cases is to say politely, "I'm sorry, but my lawyer has told me to answer fully and openly any questions about child care or my relationship with the children, but not to discuss other issues. Could we move on to the next question?"

If you're concerned about the possibility of inappropriate questions, be sure to discuss strategy in advance with your lawyer. If you've decided how to respond and practiced your answers, you'll handle the situation more smoothly should it occur. Then, if possible, redirect the conversation to child care issues.

Usually the children aren't interviewed as part of the custody process, because it's recognized that the interviews could be stressful for them. Sometimes, though, a social worker or other trained interviewer will talk to the children to get their views. Most make a real effort to be nonthreatening, often using a playroom for the talk and avoiding direct, intrusive questions.

If your children are interviewed, you can help by letting them know they don't have to be afraid. Explain that this is a counselor who is helping Mom and Dad and the judge, and that they can help by telling about their lives. If they seem anxious, ask them why. They may need reassurance that you and their father will love them whatever they say.

Often there's a temptation to try to coach or control the

children to say the "right" things. If you find yourself tempted, don't do it. It's a terrible burden on the child, who feels torn by conflicting loyalties and adult expectations.

It also, incidentally, is as likely to backfire as to work. Children aren't good at remembering coached statements, and a skilled interviewer can tell when a child has been coached. Only a child who has been terrorized into believing a viewpoint—the so-called brainwashed child—can persist in stating a coached viewpoint, and you don't want to do that to your child.

If you're afraid that the children's father has been coaching or pressuring the children, it might be helpful to use the "What if . . ." game described in Chapter 7 to explore the issue. After starting the game with less serious examples, you could ask, "What if an adult wanted you to say things that weren't true, or that you didn't believe? And what if that adult was someone you really liked a lot?"

If you find that the children are anxious about the issue, you can reassure them. You can explain that they don't have to obey a request like that, and that you're so proud of them when they tell the truth. You also can explain that sometimes adults make mistakes, and telling a child to lie or keep secrets would be a bad mistake. A caring adult might make that mistake but, after thinking about it later, would also be proud if the child told the truth anyway.

Notice that you haven't put the children in the middle by asking if their father is the one who's made that "mistake." (If they mention him, fine, but don't do so first.) You've relieved the children from any burden of being asked to speak against you, but not by asking them to speak against their father. At the same time, you've helped make sure that coaching by the father won't corrupt the interview process.

Once all the interviews are complete, the social worker or other investigator will make a written report to the judge. Usually, the report will include a custody recommendation, which the judge may or may not follow. Both lawyers will see a copy of the report, but in most states, the parents themselves will not. You can get general information about the content of the report from your lawyer, and your lawyer can object to any information in it that is inaccurate or unrelated to child-raising issues.

THE CUSTODY HEARING

After the custody investigation is complete, the judge holds a hearing in which both parents, acting through their attorneys, may present evidence and arguments as to why they should have custody.

Ordinarily, neither parent charges the other with unfitness, but each asserts that he or she would be the best custodian. Yet since few states offer much guidance to judges in making this choice (beyond the vague standard that the choice should be "in the best interests of the child"), a wide range of evidence may be allowed. While evidence generally is presented about past caregiving patterns and parent-child relationships, evidence about lifestyle is also common. Not infrequently, issues of values and personal opinion, such as those described in Chapter 6, can dilute the focus on child care issues.

An occasional parent will claim that the other parent is "unfit." Often this is done simply to be dramatic and to get the judge's attention. As a practical matter, it means only that the accusing parent will try to show the other parent's failings and flaws—which is probably what would have happened anyway.

In fact, unfitness is rarely proved, for an important reason. While exact standards vary by state, unfitness usually involves extreme abuse or neglect of the children. So, when it is charged, it is invariably combined with the milder custody claim based on the best interests of the children. Then, routinely, the judge's final order states that both parents are fit custodians, but chooses one "in the best interests of the children."

Frequently, the custody hearing is combined with a hearing on other divorce or separation issues, such as financial matters or, occasionally, grounds for divorce. Here, however, we'll focus on custody issues only.

Most of the evidence presented at a custody hearing will be individual testimony, given under oath. You can expect to testify at the hearing, as will the children's father.

There will be two main parts to your testimony. In the *direct examination*, your lawyer will ask you open-ended questions in a direct and courteous manner. For example: "Who usually did the cooking during your marriage?" In the *cross-examination*, the children's father's lawyer will ask you questions designed to get you to agree with the father's version of the facts. For example: "Now, isn't it true that Mr. X [the father] has always done a great deal of the cooking, even though he held a full-time job and you didn't?"

That form of questioning is intimidating only until you get used to it. You don't have to agree with the lawyer, even if a statement is partially true. You can calmly disagree and clarify: "No, that's not really accurate. Before I was employed, I did almost all the cooking. When I began working part time, my husband began cooking some breakfasts and Saturday night dinner, but I still did most of the cooking."

If you are cut off from giving a complete answer during the cross-examination, don't worry. Your lawyer can come back for the *redirect examination*. Then you can explain fully, under the sympathetic questioning of your lawyer.

As always, practice in advance helps. Since lawyers know the cross-examination technique better than your friends do (even those who've watched Perry Mason), you could have your lawyer ask you some likely questions.

An important factor strengthening your testimony will be the diary you've been keeping about the care of the children. Judges know that while most people won't actually lie in court, they may remember selectively, exaggerate, or change their perceptions over time to suit their own best interests. Your diary, on the other hand, is filled with facts, recorded as they actually happened. As you use it to "refresh your memory," you'll paint a reliable, believable picture of your life with the children.

It's also helpful to have other witnesses, who can describe your primary and positive role with the children. Start thinking now about whom you could ask to be a witness. Close friends and family members are an obvious possibility, but the judge may disregard them as biased. (If a member of the father's family will testify on your behalf, that, of course, is strong evidence—but due to family loyalty, it's unlikely to happen.)

Teachers, day care providers, and health care workers all can be excellent witnesses. If you've been the one to bring and pick up the children, to discuss any problems, and to leave work if a child is sick, these are the people who can confirm that. If you've been out of touch with any of them lately, begin now to reestablish contact.

Possibly, the mental health professional who conducted the custody investigation will be included as a witness in the case. (This varies by area; in many courts, the written report alone is used.) If so, cross-examination of the investigator can help to reveal possible oversights or biases in the report.

Sometimes *expert witnesses* are used to testify about matters that generally aren't understood by laypeople. In custody cases, mental health professionals are most often called in. Some common uses of an expert witness in a custody case include:

- Explaining the importance of maintaining the child's relationship with the primary caregiver.
- Explaining that a nontraditional lifestyle choice by a parent (such as homosexuality or lack of church attendance) is of less importance to the child's well-being than the parent-child relationship.
- Explaining that it would not be in the children's best interests to grant custody to a father who had been violent toward the children's mother.
- Testifying, based on observations of the children and/or meetings with one or both parents, as to the expert's perception of the parent-child relationships.

(Frequently, the parent not recommended in the custody investigation will seek an outside expert to disagree with the investigator's findings.)

Unfortunately, expert witnesses are generally expensive. Talk with your lawyer about expected costs, and consider checking with local community health centers or child guidance clinics to see if there are experts who can help at a lower fee.

Just as you'll be using your own testimony and that of other witnesses to establish your case, so will the children's father. You may be worried that the father or his witnesses will not be honest. While that's possible, outright lying really is not common. More often, witnesses exaggerate a little or are deliberately vague. With careful questioning, your lawyer can get a more accurate account.

Probably the most common area of exaggeration is the father's role in child raising, which in turn can be misunderstood by the judge. Because most men never have had total responsibility for child raising, they may not realize how much work is involved. The father may describe a few tasks he has regularly performed and (believing it to be only a slight exaggeration) testify that child care is shared equally. The judge (usually a middle-aged man with even less child-raising experience) may believe that the few duties really do represent an equal share.

There is a very effective way to combat this problem. Your lawyer can ask the father a series of detailed questions about the children's lives and their care—teachers' names, clothing sizes, food preferences, interests, friends, and so on. Later, you will be asked the same or similar questions. Your answers will show how involved each of you truly is.

An excellent resource your lawyer can and should use is the handbook *Representing Primary Caretaker Parents in Custody Disputes* (see Appendix A). It contains, among other resources, a list of over four hundred questions relating to child care. Because it's so detailed, it shows not only how involved each parent is, but also just how much work really is involved in raising a child.

A more serious problem occurs when an expert witness twists the truth or cites as "facts" opinions that most reputable professionals would reject. Tragically, while most mental health experts are ethical and honest, there are always those (as in any profession) who will express any opinion for a high enough fee. Psychologist Deborah Anna Luepnitz of the Philadelphia Child Guidance Clinic tells of being assured she could "name her fee" if she would aid the joint custody bid of a man who admittedly had sexually molested the child in the past. She flatly refused—but another expert was found who did not refuse.

Your best defense against an unethical expert is an ethical one who will testify and disagree. It's also helpful to have your lawyer question the adverse expert in court about the full fee paid, including consultation before the hearing, because an unusually high fee can raise the judge's suspicions. If there have been disciplinary actions against the expert in the past (you can find out from the state disciplinary board for the expert's profession), your lawyer can raise them at the hearing.

Finally, the expert should be carefully questioned about leading studies or treatises which discredit the opinion offered. For example, a mental health professional who said that children easily adapt to changes in custody should be asked about the authorities discussed in Chapter 4. One who claimed that "mildly" sexual behavior toward a child was not harmful should be asked about works such as Judith Herman's *Father-Daughter Incest.*

Lawyers preparing for the hearing may use a process called *discovery* to learn what testimony and other evidence the opposing side will be presenting. The two most common discovery tools are *interrogatories* (written questions) and the *deposition* (cross-examination of a witness before the hearing).

If you are asked to participate in a deposition, you should prepare for it just as carefully as you would for the actual hearing. If you say something that hurts your case during the deposition, you could be quizzed about it later in court.

Basically, your goals during the hearing process will be to direct the judge's attention to child care issues, to demonstrate your role as an active and loving parent, to offer evidence about any serious problems in the father-child relationship, and to refute evidence used against you. This will help set the stage for a custody order in your favor.

THE PERMANENT ORDER

When the custody investigation and hearing process are completed, the judge will issue a final order granting custody to one parent or to the parents jointly.

Actually, the order is permanent only in the relative sense. A dissatisfied parent can appeal it to a higher court, which could possibly overturn it. Additionally, the judge who issues the permanent order could later modify it if there is a significant change of circumstances.

The permanent order should be in writing, and should explain the judge's reasons. Since judges don't always offer a full explanation, your lawyer should request in advance that the reasoning be included. That way, if the order does go against you, your lawyer will have more to work with if you decide to appeal.

The order should also specify frequency and approximate length of visitation by the noncustodial parent. This protects parents and children from a continuing fight over the meaning of the vague phrase that judges sometimes use: "The noncustodial parent shall have reasonable visitation."

THE APPEAL

If you do lose custody in the permanent order, you can appeal the decision to a higher court. In most cases, the permanent order will be in effect until the higher court makes its decision. The only exception is when the temporary custody order was different, and the judge who issues the permanent order agrees to leave the temporary order in effect until the higher court makes its decision.

In order to appeal, your lawyer must object to a legal error the judge made. The claim "My client would have been a better custodian" would not in itself be grounds for an appeal, because this is a matter of judgment within the judge's discretion. However, the claim "The judge failed to give adequate consideration to my client's primary role in child raising, while overemphasizing financial considerations" would be grounds for an appeal. The more strongly prior cases within the state had emphasized the requirement that judges consider past child raising, the more likely the appeal would be to succeed.

Often, deciding whether to appeal an adverse custody order is as difficult as deciding whether to go to court in the first place. Although neither you nor your children will have an active role in the appeal (which is handled, mostly on paper, by your lawyer), it still can prolong the anxiety of not knowing what will happen. Cost is also a continuing concern. Finally, many women fear that a higher court will automatically support the lower court judge's decision.

While it is possible to win an appeal, it's true that the chances are not good. A study of appeals court cases reported in 1982 showed that of the fifty-two mothers who appealed an award of custody granted to the children's father, only ten (19 percent) succeeded in reversing the award.[42] Practicing lawyers, in general, confirm this bleak view.

Nonetheless, if you can afford to appeal, there are some good reasons to consider it. If you truly fear for the children's welfare with their father (for example, if there is a history of abuse, which the judge didn't believe), any chance of regaining custody may be better than none.

Sometimes it's also important to appeal an unfair decision at least partly on moral grounds, in hopes of gradually improving the law. State appeals courts are where the state law is interpreted, shaped, and defined. If they see only appeals from wealthy fathers, and none from poor mothers, they could end up considering only the wealthy fathers' concerns.

Judges could swing increasingly toward protecting the rights of the wealthy and powerful, while ignoring the concern of parents who have spent their energies raising the children instead of raising their salaries. And since children benefit more from parental caretaking than from parent power, the children would suffer most.

MODIFICATION ACTIONS

Even after the custody decision is final and any appeal concluded, there is one more way that custody may be changed. Either party can bring an action for *modification* of the custody order. In fact, modification actions are more common than initial custody disputes. The most common form of modification action appears to be that of a father (often one who initially agreed that the mother should have custody) who requests a change of custody.

The procedure for a modification action is largely similar to the regular custody process. While there is usually no need for a temporary order (since the old order is already in effect), the custody investigation, hearing, final order, and appeal process are much the same as in an initial case.

There are a few differences, but they tend to be more technical than actual. In most states, judges are not supposed to consider a modification action unless there has been a substantial *change of circumstance* in the child's present home. Also, the parent who wants the custody change is supposed to have the burden of proving that circumstances have changed, and that it would be in the children's best interests for custody to be switched.

These rules have been developed because it's generally recognized that unnecessary custody switches can hurt children. Unfortunately, judges tend to apply the rules very loosely, and have been criticized for switching custody too easily.[43] In fact, custodial mothers who face a modification challenge may actually lose custody at a higher rate than mothers challenged at divorce time.[44]

Sometimes, fathers have sought the custody modifications because of serious, even dangerous, problems in the mother's home. In these cases, the custody modifications are probably a good thing.

More often, however, custody modification actions involve the lifestyle judgments discussed in Chapter 6. A few years after a divorce, many men have settled into the traditional life that judges like so much: remarriage, a stable career, and a suburban lifestyle. Most custodial mothers are still on their own, juggling child care demands, an entry-level job, and the constant fight against poverty.

If you do face a modification action, be sure to use the strategies discussed in Chapter Six. More than ever, you'll want to stress continuity of care. In one respect, your task will be easier, because the fact that you've had custody since the divorce makes it clear that you are the primary caretaker. If the father tries to exaggerate his past involvement with the children, however, you'll still have to use techniques such as referring to your child care diary and having your lawyer quiz him about the children's daily lives.

The court process, however hostile it may sometimes seem, really is intended as a fact-finding method. If you go to court over custody, it's because you have strong reasons to believe that your children will benefit from having you as a custodian. These are the reasons that you, with your lawyer, will present. Whatever happens, you'll have the satisfaction of knowing that you did your best.

9 □ BEGINNING TO HEAL

In Sue Miller's beautifully written novel, *The Good Mother* (Harper & Row, 1986), the main character is a woman who loses custody of her four-year-old daughter. Devastated by the judge's decision, she nonetheless feels she must put on a happy face for her daughter. Although the child clings to her and begs to stay with her mother, the mother holds back her tears and insists that the decision is for the best. She never explains that she, too, wishes that the child could stay, but that they must obey the judge's order. The child is left feeling deserted, convinced that her mother doesn't want her.

The mother's decision to hide her own grief undoubtedly springs from a noble instinct. Throughout the proceedings, she has carefully avoided voicing any anger toward the child's father in her presence. This loving gesture has been crucial to helping the child through a difficult time, because angry criticisms of a parent can only cause pain and confusion. That habit of silence, however, carries over into a time when carefully worded frankness might be better.

If you do lose custody of your child or are unhappy with court-ordered custody arrangements, you can be honest without being divisive. It is fine to tell your children, "Your father and I both love you very much, and we each wanted you with us as much as possible. Since we couldn't agree, we asked a judge to help us, and the judge decided that you should live with your father most of the time. I'm very sad, because I'll miss you, but I also know that there will be some good things for you about the new arrangement. We'll still be together often, and I'll always be here if you need me or have a problem. Anyway, now that it's decided, let's try to find ways to make the plan work as well as possible."

However a custody dispute is resolved, there will always be a need for all parties involved to heal and begin anew. You've been through a traumatic time, with upheaval and uncertainty. You and your children will need tenderness, patience, and nurturance. You can get that through reaching out to friends and perhaps to a therapist and/or support group. One important resource, if you've lost custody, may be a support group of Mothers without Custody (see Appendix C for a referral network). Talking to others who understand your feelings can help you find comfort and strength.

Life after divorce is a new phase of your life with your children. Whatever the custody plan, your relationship with each child remains key to that child's emotional welfare and growth. Be as active and involved as you can, within the limits of the custody plan.

If your parenting responsibility is decreased after the divorce (voluntarily or involuntarily), you might find you have new time and energy to devote to your career and personal development. Embrace the opportunity. Many women, coming out of the crisis of divorce, experience dramatic gains in career achievement and satisfaction. That can only improve your life and, indirectly, that of your children. Career stability will also be helpful for avoiding future custody conflicts.

In the spring of 1986, a conference was held in New York City called "Mothers on Trial: The Politics of Child Custody." In a workshop, mothers who had been or were involved in custody disputes gathered together to learn and support one another. Their voices were gentle, sometimes sad, but still filled with love and life. Although their comments were individual, their message blended together:

Talk to your children. Let them know that you'll always love them, no matter what happens.
Let them be sad. Let them be angry, even angry with you.

If they can show their hurt and anger, it's because they trust you.

If you do lose custody, it will be painful to see your children for a day or two, then say goodbye for the week. See them anyway. After a while, new routines will develop. It doesn't stop hurting, but it gets better.

One woman attended with the sixteen-year-old daughter whose custody she'd lost several years before. Now old enough to decide for herself, the girl had elected to return to her mother's home. She added her own advice:

The judge can decide whether your kids will live with you, but not how much you'll love them. Just keep loving them, whatever happens, and they'll know in their hearts they can count on you.

Notes

1. See Judith Wallerstein and Joan Kelly, *Surviving the Breakup: How Children and Parents Cope with Divorce* (New York: Basic Books, 1980).

2. Leonore Weitzman, *The Divorce Revolution: The Unexpected Social and Economic Consequences for Women and Children in America* (New York: The Free Press, 1985), p. 233, table 22, 1977 figures. This study is the most accurate indicator of overall male and female success rates, because it is based on a random sampling of all divorce cases in the jurisdiction studied. Two other studies, based not on random samples but on selected populations, include:

- Phyllis Chesler's in-depth study of sixty mothers who had been the children's primary caretakers prior to divorce, and who were involved in a custody dispute. Seventy percent of these mothers lost custody. The study population included women who were referred by private therapists, other professionals, or other study participants; as well as women who responded to an advertisement seeking "mothers who had been involved in a custody dispute" or who contacted the interviewer in seeking a custody expert. See Phyllis Chesler, *Mothers on Trial: The Battle for Children and Custody* (New York: McGraw-Hill, 1986).
- Jeff Atkinson's statistical study of appellate cases reported nationwide in 1982. Out of a total of 204 cases, the final custody result after the appeals court ruled was 105 (51 percent) to the father and 99 (49 percent) to the mother. However, the trial courts were much more likely to award custody to the father: At that level, 127 (62 percent) of the fathers and 77 (38 percent) of the mothers received custody. For more on this study, see note 29.

These studies, designed primarily to examine the reasons for custody decisions, were each based on a group that may not have represented the population as a whole. Chesler's population comprised mothers willing to discuss past custody conflicts. Possibly, mothers who had won custody would feel less of a need to discuss it, and more of a desire to put the experience behind them. This may be one reason why the women in the study were somewhat more likely to have lost custody than in Weitzman's study.

Atkinson's statistical study included only cases that had been appealed and reported. Women who lost custody but couldn't afford to appeal their cases (which probably includes most women who lose custody at the trial level) are not included. This may explain the somewhat lower—but still better than even—rate of male custody success in the study.

Weitzman's study, comprising a random sample of the total divorcing populations, has neither of these limitations. For this reason, it is used in the text to give a general view of male and female success rates.

3. *The 1985 Virginia Slims American Women's Opinion Poll: A Study Conducted by The Roper Organization, Inc.*, p. 93, table 6.8. Available from The Roper Center, University of Connecticut, Storrs, CN 06268.

4. *New York Times*, November 1, 1980. See also John Robinson, *How Americans Use Time: A Social-Psychological Analysis* (New York: Holt Rinehart & Winston/Praeger Books, 1977).

5. See, for example, David Lynn, *The Father: His Role in Child Development* (Belmont, Cal.: Wadsworth, 1974); M. Lamb, ed., *The Role of the Father in Child Development* (New York: John Wiley & Sons, 1976); Wisdom, "The Role of the Father in the Minds of Parents, in Psychoanalytic Theory and in the Life of the Infant," *International Review of Psychoanalysis* 3 (1976).

6. Nancy Polikoff, "Why Mothers Are Losing: A Brief Analysis of Criteria Used in Child Custody Determinations," *Women's Rights Law Reporter* 7: 235 (1982).

7. Ibid.

8. See Chapter 4 and the authorities cited in notes 30–33 below.

9. See note 1 above.

10. See, e.g., Weitzman, *The Divorce Revolution*, pp. 250, 253–56.

11. Diana Russell, in *Rape in Marriage* (New York: Macmillan, 1982), reported that 21 percent of a randomly selected group of 644 ever-married women reported that they had at some point been subjected to physical violence by their husbands. Other studies reporting higher rates are reported in Lenore Walker, *The Battered*

Woman (New York: Harper & Row, 1979); and Strauss, Gelles, and Steinmetz, *Behind Closed Doors: Violence in the American Family* (New York: Doubleday Anchor, 1980).

12. See National Center on Child Abuse and Neglect, *Executive Summary: National Study of the Incidence and Severity of Child Abuse and Neglect* (Washington, D.C.: U.S. Government Printing Office).

13. See Strauss, "Ordinary Violence, Child Abuse, and Wife-Beating: What Do They Have in Common?" in *The Dark Side of Families*, ed. David Finklehor, et al. (Beverly Hills: Sage Publications, 1983). Also see, e.g., *Pikula* v. *Pikula*, 374 N.W.2d 705 (1985).

14. See Louise Armstrong, "Daddy Dearest," *Connecticut*, January 1984.

15. Reported in Chesler, *Mothers on Trial*, p. 68 and accompanying note 8.

16. Louis Keifer, *How to Win Custody* (Cornerstone, 1982). Keifer's presentation of kidnapping techniques is offered not in the context of fleeing from violence (as a portion of this book is), but for any father who disagrees with a judge's final decision. In fact, the only mention of violence in Keifer's presentation is violence by the kidnapping father. In an example, Keifer tells of a man who, shortly before kidnapping his child, hired a friend to beat the child's mother and inform her she would never see the child again. Keifer does not question this violent man's suitability as his child's custodian, but presents the tale in a "humorous" vein.

17. Weitzman, *The Divorce Revolution*, pp. 54–61.

18. Polikoff, "Why Mothers Are Losing."

19. Ibid. See also Chesler, *Mothers on Trial*, p. 84.

20. Bureau of the Census, *Child Support and Alimony: 1983*, Special Studies, Series P-23, table 3.

21. Ibid., table 1.

22. Weitzman, *The Divorce Revolution*, p. 323.

23. Ibid., p. 31.

24. Ibid., pp. 224, 310–18.

25. Joan Wexler, "Rethinking the Modification of Child Custody Decrees," *Yale Law Journal* 94:757 (1985).

26. Ibid.

27. This statement is based on analysis of the data contained in: Jeff Atkinson, "Criteria for Deciding Child Custody in the Trial and Appellate Courts," *Family Law Quarterly* 18 (1984). Atkinson compiled data on custody cases appealed to state appeals courts in

1982. These included two sets of cases:

- *Initial determinations*—cases in which custody was being decided for the first time. In the trial court, the judge granted custody to 52 (58 percent) of the fathers and 38 (42 percent) of the mothers. On appeal, several of the awards were reversed, so the final total was custody to 44 (49 percent) of the fathers and 46 (51 percent) of the mothers.
- *Modification actions*—cases in which custody had been previously held by one parent, by court order or agreement, but which the other parent now challenged. In most of these cases (83 percent), the mother had had custody since the divorce, so that technically the father should have had the burden of proving that a change would be in the children's best interest.

  Despite that fact, the fathers were more likely to win than the mothers who had been caring for the children—or than the fathers who were seeking initial determinations. Among the modification actions, trial court judges awarded custody to the father in 75 (66 percent) of cases and to the mother in 39 (34 percent). Again, several custody awards were reversed on appeal, so the final total was custody to 61 (54 percent) of fathers and to 53 (46 percent of mothers).

Surprisingly, Atkinson uses his data to argue that *fathers* are discriminated against in custody decisions. He does this by adding together the appellate decisions for both modifications and initial determinations and noting that fathers win in 51 percent of cases. He then: (1) notes that it is "possible" that mothers actually win more often, perhaps because losing fathers are advised by their lawyers not to appeal, or perhaps because appeals courts fail to report cases in which mothers win; (2) overlooks the possibility that many losing mothers cannot afford to appeal; (3) overlooks the possibility that mothers have been more involved than fathers in child raising during the marriage; (4) overlooks the fact (buried within his own figures) that most of the modification actions involved children whose custody had been with their mother since the divorce; and (5) overlooks the fact (also indicated by his figures) that women were more likely to lose at the trial court level in both initial determinations and modification actions.

28. See Polikoff, "Why Mothers Are Losing," for an excellent discussion of historical trends.

29. See Weitzman, *The Divorce Revolution,* for a comprehensive analysis of the effects of no-fault divorce on women and children.

30. Bowlby, *Attachment and Loss:* Vol. I, *Attachment* (1969); Vol. II, Separation (1973); Vol. III, *Loss* (1980) (New York: Basic Books).

31. Goldstein, Freud, and Solnit, *Beyond the Best Interests of the Child* (New York: The Free Press, 1984) (reprinted edition).

32. Lamb, "Effects of Stress and Cohort on Mother- and Father-Infant Interaction," *Dev. Psychology* 13:435 (1976), 441–42; Ainsworth, "Infant-Mother Attachment," *American Psychologist* 34:932 (1979).

33. See, e.g., M. Rutter, *The Qualities of Mothering: Material Deprivation Reassessed* (Aronson Books, 1974).

34. Weitzman, *The Divorce Revolution,* p. 323.

35. Bureau of the Census, *Child Support and Alimony: 1983,* Special Studies, Series P-23, p. 2.

36. U.S. Department of Labor, Women's Bureau, *The Employment of Women, General Diagnosis of Developments and Issues,* April 1980.

37. Weitzman, *The Divorce Revolution,* pp. 244, 310.

38. The Domestic Relations Tax Act of 1984.

39. Under the provisions of the Tax Reform Act of 1986, capital gains on a sale of a house or condominium are taxed as ordinary income, up to a maximum rate of 28 percent. You could avoid this tax by buying a new house with the proceeds, but you might not be able to afford a new house.

40. *Investigators Guide to Missing Child Cases* (National Center for Missing and Exploited Children, 1985), p. 10.

41. Report of the Police Foundation and National Institute of Justice, conducted in cooperation with the Minneapolis Police Department, 1981–82. Available from the Police Foundation, Washington, D.C.

42. Atkinson, "Criteria for Deciding Child Custody in the Trial and Appellate Courts," *Family Law Quarterly* 18 (1984).

43. Wexler, "Rethinking the Modification of Child Custody Decrees," *Yale Law Journal* 94:757 (1985).

44. See note 27 above.

Appendix A

RECOMMENDED READING

All material listed here is selected for quality of content, currency, and to address a specific area not fully covered by this book. Books from major publishers can be ordered from any bookstore, while smaller handbooks can be ordered from the addresses noted.

Overview of Women and Divorce

The Divorce Revolution: The Unexpected Social and Economic Consequences for Women and Children in America, by Lenore J. Weitzman (New York: The Free Press, 1985). The landmark study of divorce law today and its devastating effect on women and children.

Mothers on Trial: The Battle for Children and Custody, by Phyllis Chesler (New York: McGraw-Hill, 1986). A shocking, sometimes frightening look at the lives of women who faced serious, angry custody challenges. Although the study population was based on voluntary interviews and may not represent a cross-section of all contested custody cases, this is important reading because it gets to the heart of why the worst cases happen.

The Good Mother, by Sue Miller (New York: Harper & Row, 1986). This novel, which tells the story of a mother who loses custody of her young daughter, is beautifully written and highly realistic. The mother does well in stressful circumstances, yet blames herself for everything. The lawyer rejects the possibility of negotiation and proceeds straight to trial, but his decisions are never questioned.

Practical Advice for Parents

The Safe Child Book, by Sheryll Kerns Kraizer (New York: Dell, 1985). An excellent guide to teaching your children important safety techniques.

Parental Kidnapping: How to Prevent an Abduction and What to Do if Your Child Is Abducted, by Patricia Hoff (1985). Available free from the National Center for Missing and Exploited Children, 1835 K Street, N.W., Suite 700, Washington, DC 20006. Important, detailed advice for protecting your children.

Child Support, by Marianne Takas (New York: Harper & Row, 1985). A clearly written, practical guide to the financial side of divorce or separation, with emphasis upon child support negotiation and collection. Appropriate for never-married, divorcing, or divorced mothers.

A Lesbian and Gay Parents' Legal Guide to Child Custody (1985). Available for $5 from the Anti-Sexism Committee, Bay Area Chapter of the National Lawyer's Guild, 558 Capp Street, San Francisco, CA 94110. A detailed look at the special challenges of lesbian and gay custody cases.

Practice Aids to Suggest to Your Lawyer

Representing Primary Caretaker Parents in Custody Disputes (1984). Available for $15 from the Women's Legal Defense Fund, 2000 P Street, N.W., Suite 400, Washington, DC 20036. This valuable handbook contains leading cases in support of primary caretaker custody, a detailed list of questions for determining who is the primary caretaker, and other practice materials.

Lesbian Mother Litigation Manual, by Donna Hutchins (1982). Available for $35 from the Lesbian Rights Project, 1370 Mission Street, 4th Floor, San Francisco, CA 94103. Contains detailed practice tips and strategy aids.

Child Custody and Visitation Law and Practice, 4 vols. Matthew Bender & Co., 1983). May be ordered for $320 by calling 800-223-1940. A major reference work covering all aspects of custody and visitation for the practicing lawyer.

Appendix B

LEGAL ADVOCACY RESOURCES

The following organizations can offer information and referral on difficult aspects of your case, and are active in improving the legal system. In contacting them, try to be as specific as possible in stating your requests.

Child Custody Project
Women's Legal Defense Fund
2000 P Street, N.W., Suite 400
Washington, DC 20036
(Publications list, newsletter, legal advocacy and referral)

National Women's Law Center
1616 P Street, N.W.
Washington, DC 20036
(Newsletter, legislative and policy analysis, monitoring of agency
    compliance with law)

National Center on Women and Family Law
799 Broadway, Room 402
New York, NY 10003
(Publications list, newsletter, assistance to lower-income women,
    and legal service offices)

NOW Legal Defense and Education Fund
99 Hudson Street
New York, NY 10013
(Newsletter, legislative advocacy, legal advocacy, and referral)

Center for Women Policy Studies
2000 P Street, N.W., Suite 508
Washington, DC 20036
(Legislative and program advocacy, newsletter on family violence)

Children's Defense Fund
122 C Street, N.W., Suite 400
Washington, DC 20001
(Newsletter, legislative advocacy, legal advocacy, and referral)

The Children's Foundation
815 15th Street, N.W., Suite 928
Washington, DC 20005
(Newsletter, legislative and policy advocacy)

Child Custody Project
American Bar Association
1800 M Street, N.W.
Washington, DC 20036
(Parent, lawyer, and judicial education, written materials)

Lesbian Rights Project
1370 Mission Street, 4th Floor
San Francisco, CA 94103   415/ 621-0674
(Legal advocacy and referral)

Custody Action for Lesbian Mothers
Avenue of the Art Building
1346 Chestnut Street, Room 1109   215/N.L.
Philadelphia, PA 19107
(Legal advocacy and referral)

Lesbian Mothers' National Defense Fund
P.O. Box 21567
Seattle, WA 98111   206/ 325-2643
(Legal advocacy and referral)

Appendix C

NATIONAL NETWORKS FOR SELF-HELP RESOURCES

All organizations are listed by national office. Most have local offices or chapters, which you may be able to contact directly by checking your local telephone directory. Each group listed here can help you to reach local organizations offering specialized services or emotional support which may be helpful to you and your children.

Custody Disputes, Practical and Emotional Support

Mothers Without Custody
P.O. Box 56762
Houston, TX 77256-6762
713-840-1622
(For mothers facing a custody dispute or who have lost custody.)

Child Support

The Child Support Network
c/o Parents Without Partners
7910 Woodmont Avenue, Suite 1000
Bethesda, MD 20814
800-638-8078
(For parents having trouble collecting child support.)

Violence and Abuse

National Coalition Against Domestic Violence
1500 Massachusetts Avenue, N.W., Suite 35
Washington, DC 20006
202-293-8860
(Referral to local services for abused women and children.)

National Coalition Against Sexual Assault
c/o Volunteers of America
8787 State Street, Suite 202
East St. Louis, IL 62203
618-398-7764
(Referral to local services for rape victims.)

Child Help, USA
P.O. Box 630
Hollywood, CA 90028
800-422-4453
(For adults abused as children, referral to local incest survivor sup-
    port groups. For children who have been abused and their
    parents, crisis intervention and referral to local organizations
    that can help. Concerned children welcome to call.)

Parental Kidnapping

National Center for Missing and Exploited Children
1835 K Street, N.W., Suite 700
Washington, DC 20006
202-634-9821
800-834-5678 (emergency hot line)
(Referral to local action group; excellent free written materials)

Child Find, Inc.
P.O. Box 277
New Paltz, NY 12561
914-255-1848
(Assistance in locating children, referral to local attorneys and sup-
    port groups)

Alcohol Abuse

Alcoholics Anonymous World Services
P.O. Box 459
Grand Central Station
New York, NY 10163
212-686-1100
(For persons concerned about their own drinking)

Al-Anon Family Groups World Headquarters
1 Park Avenue
New York, NY 10016
212-683-1771
(For persons concerned about the drinking of a friend or family
    member, or who feel past family alcohol use has affected them)

Parenting

Parents Without Partners
8807 Colesville Road
Silver Spring, MD 20910
800-638-8078
301-588-9354
(Social and educational programs for single parents)

Parents Anonymous
22330 Hawthorne Boulevard, Suite 208
Torrance, CA 90505
213-371-3501
(For parents having difficulty controlling their anger with their chil-
    dren, who want help and support from other parents)

Appendix D

REFERENCES TO THE UNIFORM CHILD CUSTODY JURISDICTION ACT (UCCJA), CRIMINAL PARENTAL KIDNAPPING LAWS, AND THE PARENT LOCATOR SERVICE IN EVERY STATE

The numbers listed in the second and third columns tell you what section of the state Civil Code and Criminal Code (Penal Code) contains these laws. The easiest way to get a copy of *your* state's UCCJA and parental kidnapping laws is to ask your lawyer for a copy. Also, you can probably get a copy by going to a large law library. Law schools, state and federal courts, and bar associations usually maintain comprehensive law libraries. Call and ask to speak with the law librarian. Give the law librarian the citation to the UCCJA or the parental kidnapping law. Ask the librarian if the library has the volume of the state Civil or Criminal Code that contains these sections. (Remember to check for the Criminal Code for the state from which the child was taken *and* the state to which the child was taken.) If the law library has these volumes, ask if you would be permitted to use the library. If you are, the librarian may be able to help you locate the correct volume.

STATE	UNIFORM CHILD CUSTODY JURISDICTION ACT (UCCJA)	CRIMINAL PARENTAL KIDNAPPING LAWS	STATE PARENT LOCATOR SERVICE
Alabama	§§30-3-20 to 44	§13A-6-45	(205) 261-2872
Alaska	§§25.30.010-.910	§11.41.320; §11.41.330	(907) 276-3441
Arizona	§§8-401 to 424	§13-1302	(602) 255-3465
Arkansas	§§34-2701 to 2726	§41-2411	(501) 371-2464
California	§§5150-5174; §4604	§§277-279	(916) 739-5127
Colorado	§§14-13-101 to 126	§18-3-304	(303) 866-2422

Connecticut	§§46b-90 to 114	§53a-97; §53a-98	(203) 566-5438
Delaware	Title 13, §§1901-1925	Title 11, §785	(302) 421-8328
District of Columbia	Title 16, §§4501-4524		(202) 887-0364
Florida	§§61.1302-1348	§787.03; §787.04	(904) 487-3689
Georgia	§§74-501 to 525	§16-5-45	(404) 894-5945
Hawaii	§§583-1 to 26	§707-726; §707-727	(808) 548-5779
Idaho	§§5-1001 to 1025	§18-4501	(208) 334-4419
Illinois	Chapter 40, §§2101-2126	Chapter 38, §10-5	(217) 785-1970
Indiana	§§31-1-11.6-1 to 24	§35-42-3-3	(317) 232-4936
Iowa	§§598A.1-.25	§710-5; §710-6	(515) 281-4692
Kansas	§§38-1301 to 1326	§21-3422; §21-3422(a)	(913) 296-3375
Kentucky	§§403.400-.630	§509-070	(502) 564-2244
Louisiana	§§13:1700-:1724	§14.45; §14-45.1	(504) 342-4788
Maine	Title 19, §§801-825	Title 17A, §303	(207) 289-2886
Maryland	FL §§9-201 to 9-224	FL §9-301; §9-304 to §9-307	(301) 576-5474
Massachusetts	209B, §§1-14	265, §26A	(617) 574-0310
Michigan	§§600.651-.673	§28.582 (1)	(517) 373-8640
Minnesota	§§518A.01-25	§609.26	(612) 297-1113
Mississippi	§§93-23-1 to 47	§97-3-53; §97-5-5; §97-3-51	(601) 354-0341
Missouri	§§452.440-.550	§565.150	(314) 751-4301

STATE	UNIFORM CHILD CUSTODY JURISDICTION ACT (UCCJA)	CRIMINAL PARENTAL KIDNAPPING LAWS	STATE PARENT LOCATOR SERVICE
Montana	§§40-7-101 to 125	§45-5-304; §27-1-515	(406) 444-4674
Nebraska	§§43-1201 to 1225	§28-316	(402) 471-9361
Nevada	§§125A.010-.250	§200.359	(702) 885-4143
New Hampshire	§§458A:1-:25	§633.2; §633.3; §633.4	(603) 271-4438
New Jersey	§§2A:34-28 to 52	§2c:13-4	(609) 633-6259
New Mexico	§§40-10-1 to 24	§30-4-4	(505) 827-4230
New York	§§75-a to z	§135.45; §135.50	(518) 474-1070
North Carolina	§§50A-1 to 25	§14-320.1; §14-41; §14-42	(919) 733-4120
North Dakota	§§14-14-01 to 26	§14-14-22.1	(701) 224-3584
Ohio	§§3109.21-.37	§2905.04; §2919.23	(614) 466-3233
Oklahoma	Title 10, §§1601-1627	Title 21, §891	(405) 424-7572
Oregon	§§109.700-.930	§163.245; §163.257	(503) 373-7300
Pennsylvania	Title 42, §§5341-5366	Title 18, §2904	(717) 783-3032
Rhode Island	§§15-14-1 to 26	§11.26-1.1	(401) 277-2847
South Carolina	§§20-7-782 to 830	§16-17-495	(803) 758-5517
South Dakota	§§26-5-5 to 52	§29.19.7; §22.19.9; §22.19.10; §22.19.11	(605) 773-3641
Tennessee	§§36-1301 to 1325	§39-2-301; §39-2-303	(615) 741-7923

Texas	V.T.C.A. Family Code, §§11.51-11.75	§25.03; §25.04	(512) 475-5051
Utah	§§78-45c-1 to 26	§76-5-303	(801) 486-1812
Vermont	Title 15, §§1031 to 1051	Title 13, §2451	(802) 271-2756
Virgin Islands	Title 16, §§115-139		(809) 773-8240
Virginia	§§20-125 to 146	§18.2-47; §18.2-49; §18.2-50	(804) 281-9074
Washington	§§26.27.010-.930	§§9A.40.060, .070, .080	(206) 459-6454
West Virginia	§§48-10-1 to 26		(304) 348-3780
Wisconsin	§§822.01-.25	§946.71; §946.715	(608) 266-0252
Wyoming	§§20-5-101 to 125	§6-2-20; §6-2-204	(307) 777-6554

Note: A number of states are in the process of negotiating contracts for this service with the Federal Parent Locator Service. If your state does not have a contract as of this writing, contact your State Parent Locator Service to determine if your state has subsequently entered into a contract.

If you have any trouble reaching the State Parent Locator Service, call or write to the Federal Parent Locator Service:

> Federal Parent Locator Service
> Office of Child Support Enforcement
> Department of Health and Human Services
> 6110 Executive Boulevard, Rockville, MD 20850
>
> 301-443-4950

Appendix D is reprinted from *Parental Kidnapping: How to Prevent an Abduction and What to Do If Your Child Is Abducted,* August 1985. Reprinted by permission of the National Center for Missing and Exploited Children.

Index

Abuse of children, 4, 5–6, 9,
    26, 38, 47, 100–105, 112–
    127, 130
Adams, David, 102
Adult children of alcoholics,
    24–25
Adult incest survivors, 25
Aid to Families with Dependent
    Children (AFDC), 91, 126
Al-Anon Family Groups, 24, 25
Alcoholics Anonymous, 24
Alimony, 8, 73–76, 81–82, 83,
    90, 122
Appeal, 144–146
    chances of winning, 145n
Attachment and Loss, 56

Bair, Emily, 78
Bar associations, 32–33, 118
Battered women's services, 24,
    26, 47, 100–103, 116–
    127. *See also* Violence
    within family
*Behind Closed Doors: Violence
    Within the American
    Family*, 6
Best interests of child, 1, 11,
    56–58, 66, 129, 139
*Beyond the Best Interests of the
    Child*, 57
Bifurcated divorce, 82–83
Bolger, William, 32

Bowlby, John, 56
Brainwashed child, 138
Budget, 35–38, 70–71, 83–84,
    90

Capital gains tax, 76–77
Change of circumstances, 146–
    147
Chesler, Phyllis, 7
Child care responsibility, 2n,
    61–66, 90–91
    documenting, 87–88, 90–91,
    140, 147
Child support, 8, 67–68, 73–
    76, 81–82, 83, 122, 132
Child Support, 70, 91
Child Support Network, The,
    30
Conduct (fault), 79–81
Continuity of care
    how to safeguard, 58–69,
    133–135, 142, 147
    importance of, 4, 56–58
Cost-of-living increase, 83
Court process, 131–147
Covenant to execute
    documents, 84
Cross examination, 140, 141
Custody blackmail, 71–72
Custody hearing, 139–144
Custody investigation, 135–139
Custody laws, types of, 129–
    131

Day care, 29, 90–91
Debts, responsibility for, 84
Dependency deduction, 83
Deposition, 143–144
Detectives, 109
Diary, 87–88, 118, 140, 147
Direct examination, 140
Disclosure of income and assets,
    47, 78–79, 84
Discovery, 143
Displaced homemaker
    programs, 29
Divorce agreement (checklist),
    83–85
Divorce, bifurcated, 82–83
Divorce, effect on child, 1n, 19,
    148–149
Divorce law, history of, 10–13
Divorce law, by state, 73, 129–
    131
Double standard, 20, 63, 80,
    86–87, 90–94

Economic disparities between
    men and women, 7–8n
Education costs, 83–84
EMERGE, 102
Emotional support, 21–28,
    148–150
Expert witnesses, 7, 97, 141–
    143

Family members, 21–22, 141
Father-Daughter Incest, 113,
    143
Fathers, involvement in child
    raising, 2–3, 53–55, 63–66
Fathers, likelihood of winning
    custody, 2–4
Fault in divorce, 79–81
Federal Bureau of Investigation
    (FBI), 109

Fees
    expert witness, 142
    lawyer, 35–38, 84
    mediator, 49–50
Finances
    budgeting, 35–38, 70–71,
        83–84
    disparity between men and
        women, 7–8, 70
    effect on custody process, 7–
        8, 71–72
    negotiating, 169–184
Florida, custody law, 130
Freud, Anna, 57
Friends, 21–22, 141
Future legal actions, 84

Gelles, Richard, 6
Goldstein, Joseph, 57

Health maintenance
    organization (HMO), 25
Hermann, Judith, 112, 117,
    143
Hidden income and assets, 47,
    78–79, 84
Homophobia, 94
Household chores, who
    performs, 2n

Idaho, custody law, 131
Incest, 5–6n, 26, 47, 100–105,
    112–127
Incest survivors, adult, 25
Income and assets, 47, 78–79,
    84
Income taxes, 76, 78–79, 83
Interrogatories, 143

Joint custody, 4–5, 43–44, 54,
    63–64, 66–69
    presumption or preference,
        130

Kidnapping, paternal, 5, 6,
    105–112
King Solomon story, 130
Kozak, Lillian, 74, 76
Kraizer, Sheryll Kerns, 104,
    106, 115–116

Law, function in society, 10
Lawyers
    cost, 35–38
    how to choose, 31–33
    types, 33–34
Legal custody rights, 55–56,
    66–69
Legal Services Corporation, 38
Lesbian mothers, 94–98
Lousiana, custody law, 130
Luepnitz, Deborah Anna, 143

Married Women's Property
    Acts, 11
Mediation, 41–52
    dangers, 43–45
    defined, 41–43
Medical expenses, 84
Men who seek primary custody,
    2–4
Mental health
    adult, 19–28
    child, 4, 19, 53, 56–57, 61–
        66, 117, 137–138
    family, 17–20
Mock trials, 30
Modification of custody, 9,
    146–147
Mothers
    lesbian, 94–98
    never married, 8–9, 91–92
    sexually active, 92–94
    working, 90–91
*Mothers on Trial: The Battle for
    Children and Custody*, 7

Mothers on Trial: The Politics
    of Child Custody
    (conference), 149
Mothers Without Custody, 29–
    30, 150

National Center for Missing and
    Exploited Children, 112
National Center on Women and
    Family Law, 45
National Organization for
    Women (NOW), 74
National Resource Center for
    Consumers of Legal
    Services, 32
Neely, Richard, 3, 7
Neglect of children, 4
Negotiation
    difference from mediation
    of custody, 53–69, 131
    of finances, 70–85
    styles among lawyers, 33–35
Neumann, Diane, 47
Never-married mothers, 8–9,
    91–92
New Hampshire, custody law,
    130
No-fault divorce laws, effect of,
    11–12, 19–81

Office of Child Support
    Enforcement, 81
Orders
    permanent, 144–145
    protective, 107, 120–122
    temporary, 132–135

Panic, avoiding, 13–16, 18–21,
    72, 129
Parenting support groups, 24
Parent Locator Service, 112,
    126
Parents Anonymous, 24

Parents Without Partners, 29, 30
Paternity establishment, 91
Permanent order, 144–145
Philadelphia Child Guidance Clinic, 143
Physical custody, 55–56, 61–66
Police assistance, 108–109, 119–123, 126–127
Polikoff, Nancy, 3
Poverty among female-headed families, 7–8, 70–72
Primary caretaker
  custody presumption or preference, 130, 145
  defined, 2
  father as, 62–63
  mother as, 2n, 53–55, 87–88, 142–143
Property division, 74–75, 83
Protective orders, 107, 121–122
Protective shelters, 124–126
Psychiatrists, 28
Psychologists, 27–28

Rape kits, 117
Reconciliation, 17–18, 84
Redetermination of custody, 9, 146–147
Redirect examination, 140
Refreshing memory (witness), 141
Religious leaders, 25
Representing Primary Caretaker Parents in Custody Disputes, 142–143

Safe Child Book, The, 104
Safety, child, 100–127
Schulman, Joanne, 45
Secrecy and privacy, 51, 94, 95–97, 113–116, 124–127

Self-help support groups, 22–25
Sex play among children, 115–116
Sexual abuse of children, 5–6n, 26, 47, 100–105, 112–127
Sexual activity, 20, 51, 80–81, 92–99
Shared child care responsibility, 61–66
Single mothers. See Never-married mothers
Social workers (MSW), 27–28
Solnit, Albert, 57
Stepmothers, 3
Supervised visitation, 122–124
Surviving the Breakup: How Children and Parents Cope with Divorce, 64

Taxes, 73, 76–79, 83
Temporary alimony, 74
Temporary order, 132–135
Testifying in court, 30, 139–144
Texas, divorce law, 73
Theory of interchangeable mothers, 3
Therapists, types, 27–28
Therapy
  family, 26, 43, 96
  group, 26
  parent-child, 27
  personal, 25–28, 149
  self-help, 22–25, 149

Unfitness (custody challenge), 4, 139

Violence within family, 5–6, 9, 24, 26, 47, 80, 100–127, 130, 134, 141
Visitation, 61–66, 144

Wage assignment, 81
Waiver of inheritance rights, 84
Wallerstein, Judith, 64
Wealth, effect on custody
    process, 7–8
Weitzman, Lenore, 70, 71
Welfare (AFDC), 91, 126
West Virginia, custody law, 130

West Virginia, Supreme Court
    of Appeals, 3
"What if . . ." game, 104–105,
    114–115, 138
Witnesses, 7, 92, 97, 134, 141
Women's centers, 29
Women's Legal Defense Fund,
    3
Working mothers, 90–91